# The REVERSE UNDERGROUND RAILROAD

## *in Ohio*

T0321063

# The
# REVERSE
## UNDERGROUND
# RAILROAD
### in Ohio

DAVID MEYERS AND ELISE MEYERS WALKER

THE
History
PRESS

Published by The History Press
Charleston, SC
www.historypress.com

First published 2022

Manufactured in the United States

ISBN 9781467150842

Library of Congress Control Number: 2021949179

*Notice*: The information in this book is true and complete to the best of our knowledge. It is offered without guarantee on the part of the authors or The History Press. The authors and The History Press disclaim all liability in connection with the use of this book.

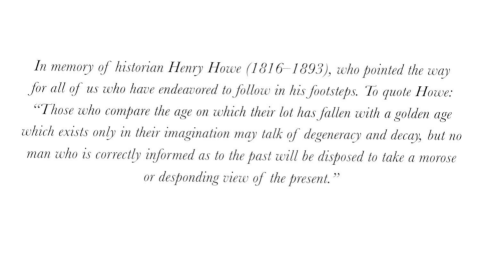

*In memory of historian Henry Howe (1816–1893), who pointed the way for all of us who have endeavored to follow in his footsteps. To quote Howe: "Those who compare the age on which their lot has fallen with a golden age which exists only in their imagination may talk of degeneracy and decay, but no man who is correctly informed as to the past will be disposed to take a morose or desponding view of the present."*

# CONTENTS

# ACKNOWLEDGEMENTS

J ohn Rodrigue and Abigail Fleming, The History Press; Dewey Scott, John Parker House; Liz Schultz, Oberlin Heritage Center; beta readers Randy McNutt and Evelyn Walker; and the Library of Congress, Wikipedia/Nyttend and Ford Walker for use of specific images.

# THE PAST IN US

*Abducting free blacks and selling them back to Southern traders became a cottage industry. Slave catchers either reaped a reward from the slave owner to whom they returned the slave, or pocketed a goodly sum—usually far more than the reward—from a slave trader to whom they sold any free black they could catch.*[1]

—*Ann Hagedorn,* Beyond the River

Slavery existed in North and South America long before there was a United States. Prior to the arrival of Europeans, some Native American tribes were known to enslave their war captives and continued to keep slaves—including African ones—well into the nineteenth century.[2] Even as the original thirteen colonies were taking shape, slave merchants were already transporting kidnapped Africans to the New World. And illegal transatlantic slave trafficking would continue until about 1870, particularly in Brazil and Cuba.

But the North American slave trade paled in comparison to that taking place nearer the equator. Beginning in the sixteenth and ending in the nineteenth century, the overwhelming majority of African slaves were shipped to Brazil and the Caribbean, according to data analysts Andrew Kahn and Jamelle Bouie. Less than 4 percent of the more than 10 million slaves brought to the Western Hemisphere—or 388,747—came to North America.

"This was dwarfed by the 1.3 million brought to Spanish Central America, the 4 million brought to British, French, Dutch, and Danish holdings in the Caribbean, and the 4.8 million brought to Brazil," they noted.[3] Though this does not absolve the United States of this stain on its history, it does underscore the fact that the newborn country was far from the only transgressor.

Trafficking in African slaves appeared as early as the eighth century when Arab Muslims purchased individuals who had already been enslaved in tribal wars to carry back to the Middle East. From the sixteenth to the nineteenth centuries, the so-called Barbary pirates—North African Muslims—raided European countries to obtain white captives for ransom or to sell into slavery in Arabia. Miguel de Cervantes, author of *Don Quixote*, was one of these slaves.

The very word *slave* is derived from the Latin *sclavus*, which means "slav"—the ethnic name for those who lived on the west coast of Bosnia on the Adriatic Sea. The slavs were, in fact, the most important source of slaves for the Muslim world during the eighth and ninth centuries. But it didn't begin then. Slavery dates back to at least 3500 BCE and continues to this day in some parts of the world.[4]

So when it comes to the institution of slavery, there is a lot of blame to go around. Even Canada had slaves. As Canadian William D. Gairdner observed, "An irony of the history of slavery in Canada is that many individual US states (Delaware, Michigan, Rhode Island, and Connecticut) had banned slavery outright twenty years before Canada prohibited (only) the future importation of slaves. So the state of Michigan…became an 'instant haven for slaves escaping from Upper Canada.'"[5]

The first Africans were brought to Virginia in 1619 after being taken from a Portuguese slave ship by an English privateer.[6] However, the English likely treated them as indentured servants, the same way they had one thousand bonded Europeans who had preceded them—at least until the laws legalizing slavery in Virginia were enacted in 1661. What became of these twenty or so individuals can only be speculated.

Massachusetts was the first colony to legalize slavery, with the passage of the ironically named "Body of Liberties" in 1641. Drafted by Nathaniel Ward, a Puritan minister, this seminal bill of rights stipulated, "There shall never be any bond slavery, villeinage, or captivity amongst us unless it be lawful captives taken in just wars, and such strangers as willing to sell themselves or are sold to us."[7] Nearly thirty years later, it was amended to include the enslavement of any child born to a slave woman as well. As a

Slave traders came to America long before there was a United States. *Library of Congress.*

result, Massachusetts would serve as the center for slave trade in the colonies throughout much of the next couple of centuries.

As early as 1772, Thomas Jefferson, James Madison and Patrick Henry—slaveholders all—had sought to have the Virginia Assembly ban the importation of slaves into the American colonies. King George III, however, overruled them. Four years later, in his first draft of the Declaration of Independence, Jefferson included language prohibiting slavery. But he removed it with reluctance when representatives from South Carolina and Georgia warned that they would not sign the document unless he did so.

Since the United States did not gain its independence from Great Britain until the Treaty of Paris in 1783, the fledgling government's first successful attempt to grapple with the issue of slavery was the Northwest Ordinance, enacted on July 13, 1787. In Article 6, it states: "There shall be neither slavery nor involuntary servitude in the said territory, otherwise than in the punishment of crimes whereof the party shall have been duly convicted."[8] However, in deference to the slaveholding interests of the newly formed nation, fugitive slaves and indentured servants who entered the territory could be "lawfully reclaimed and conveyed to the person claiming his or her labor or service as aforesaid."[9] This, then, was the first fugitive slave regulation governing the Ohio Territory.

The U.S. Constitution, effective March 4, 1789, mirrored the sentiment of the Northwest Ordinance in Article IV, although the language makes no mention of slavery per se: "No person held to service or labour in one state, under the laws thereof, escaping into another, shall, in consequence of any law or regulation therein, be discharged from such service or labor, but shall be delivered up on claim of the party to whom such service or labour may be due."[10]

As a result, this shotgun marriage of the free states and the slave was troubled from the beginning.

Just four years afterward, at the insistence of the slave states, Congress enacted the first Fugitive Slave Act on February 12, 1793, making it a crime to harbor a fugitive slave or interfere in his or her apprehension. The law required local governments to seize and return to their owners any runaway slaves found within the territorial boundaries of the United States. It applied equally to indentured servants, whether Black or white.

In 1803, Ohio became the seventeenth state admitted to the United States. By the time Kansas joined in 1861, the number of states had doubled to thirty-four. Between those two dates, thousands of fugitives from slavery crossed the Ohio River and passed through Ohio in their quest for freedom. By some estimates, more than 100,000 runaways may have actually reached the North, but the natural growth in the Black population in the Southern states more than offset any losses. Slaveholder fears that they were losing a war of attrition seem to have been overblown. But they were losing a war for the hearts and minds of the American people.

Ironically, there was no specific mention of slavery in the Constitution until the ratification of the Thirteenth Amendment in 1865—which abolished it—except in reference to "other persons" (in other words, those not free). This was despite the fact that, at the time the Constitution was enacted, an estimated one-fifth of the population of the American colonies was held in bondage.

The status of fugitive slaves varied not only from state to state but also over time with the passage of new laws and periodic court rulings. The one constant was that enslaved people continued to flee from their masters and those who sympathized with their plight sometimes helped them, giving rise to what is now known as the Underground Railroad or UGRR. Because aiding and abetting the escape of fugitive slaves was illegal, those involved in the UGRR rarely kept records. Much of its purported history was written down long afterward and must be viewed with a degree of skepticism due to both dimming memories and embroidered ones.

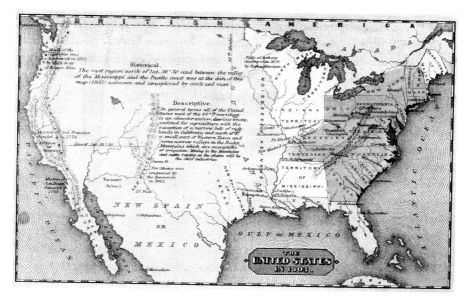

Unlike the previous sixteen, Ohio was never a slave state. *Authors' collection.*

The railroad analogy is also misleading. The routes the fugitives traveled were not hard and fast. The agents who assisted the freedom seekers were often forced to improvise in order to outwit their pursuers. To the extent that there were networks, they generally operated independently. Black conductors worked with Black conductors, white conductors with white conductors. However, in Ripley, Cincinnati, Sandusky, Oberlin and other scattered places across Ohio, history shows that they sometimes worked in concert, even at the risk of their own freedom.

Slaves, for good reason, were wary of entrusting their lives to white people, although, in time, Levi Coffin, John Rankin, John Mahan, Francis Parish and a number of others—all white—gained reputations for being trustworthy. However, those seeking freedom also needed to be careful not to blindly place their faith in all people of color. There were both Black slave owners and Black slave hunters who had no compunctions about dealing in human misery for their own economic gain.[11]

While the majority of Ohioans in the northern part of the state were against slavery, opinion was more divided in the south. Historian Carl David Schilling has estimated that as many as half of the settlers in southern Ohio were born in Southern states, mainly Virginia, Kentucky, Maryland and North Carolina. Since they occupied the counties adjacent to the Ohio River, these Southern sympathizers sometimes joined in the hunt for fugitive slaves who made their way to the Ohio shore.

Perversely, the same government that had outlawed slavery in the Northwest Territory also protected the slave owners' property rights, authorizing them to enter Ohio to retrieve fugitive slaves with near impunity. Sometimes they came in search of particular quarry, but other times it was in hope of stumbling across runaways—or persons who could be passed off as runaways. The law required little more than an accusation; legal hearings were often superficial, with the onus on the accused to prove his or her innocence.

As we discussed in *Historic Black Settlements of Ohio*, the Buckeye State became a magnet for both free Black people and those endeavoring to escape from bondage. The focus of the present work is the kidnapping of African Americans and other people of color, whether fugitives or not, in an effort to transport them back to the South—the "Reverse Underground Railroad," if you will.

Among Professor Wilbur Siebert's Underground Railroad notes was the mention of a slave catcher named McAllister—presumably Richard McAllister, a U.S. commissioner, who once bragged in a letter, "More fugitives have been remanded by me than any other U.S. Com."[12] According to Major Ephraim C. Dawes, an early historian of the Civil War, McAllister "belonged to the return line. You see the thing worked both ways."[13] Elsewhere, Siebert refers to a few others by name, but in nearly all instances they remain shadowy figures who left behind no biographies. It is perhaps fitting that most died in obscurity, because they deserved no better.

In the following pages, we have recounted many stories that illustrate how the law of the land changed throughout the period leading up to the Civil War. Some of them are familiar; others are not. Collectively, however, we hope that they provide a sense of the terror and injustice experienced by many African Americans who sought to find freedom in Ohio or beyond, while highlighting the bravery exhibited by those who risked their own freedom while endeavoring to come to their aid. It is a lesson that never should be forgotten. For as historian Ulrich Phillips observed, "We do not live in the past, but the past in us."[14]

David Meyers

*Note: We are sensitive to the fact that slave, owner, master and other such terms are reprehensible in this context. However, it is awkward to write about the institution of slavery without using them to some extent. We do not mean to be hurtful. But history can be unpleasant. And substituting another term, such as* bondservant—*which we have done on occasion for the sake of variety—somehow seems to minimize the brutality of the institution. If the contents of this book do not upset you, then we have failed to convey just how awful it was.*

*1*

# THE HUNTING OF MEN

*HAVE ye heard of our hunting, o'er mountain and glen,*
*Through cane-brake and forest,—the hunting of men?*
*—John Greenleaf Whittier, "The Hunters of Men"*[15]

In Richard Connell's popular short story "The Most Dangerous Game," a big-game hunter from New York City takes a tumble off a yacht while sailing in the Caribbean. Swimming to a nearby island, he finds it is owned by a Russian aristocrat who also enjoys hunting—hunting men, that is. What follows is a deadly game of cat-and-mouse under circumstances that differ little from the experience of many runaway slaves who fled to Ohio in the years prior to the Civil War. But, instead of Russian aristocrats, these fugitives were being hunted by slave catchers. And odd as it might seem now, these hunters of men enjoyed the protection and even the support of the law throughout the nation.

From its inception, Ohio was a free state, a state in which the "peculiar institution" of slavery—as Senator John C. Calhoun of South Carolina dubbed it—was illegal.[16] But it would prove to be freer for some than for others, and it was not strictly a matter of Black and white. This was driven home every time a fair-skinned individual deemed to be a "Negro," "mulatto" or "colored" was remanded into slavery. Some were even "whiter" than their owners. How could that be? It clearly made some white folks anxious.

As W.E.B. Du Bois observed over a century ago, "It is generally recognized today that no scientific definition of race is possible."[17] Race is merely a social construct, a short-handed way to categorize biological diversity. As such, it has been used to rationalize all manner of human atrocities, including chattel slavery in which people are treated as personal property to be bought, sold or brutalized. In short, they were regarded by their oppressors as something less than human.

Slavery had been forbidden in the Ohio Territory since 1787, but enslaved people could still be found there. It was not unusual for slave owners visiting Ohio to be accompanied by their bondservants. Some slaveholders routinely brought their slaves from Virginia and Kentucky to work the farms in Ohio's southernmost counties. And there were also fugitives from slavery who escaped to Ohio, seeking to lose themselves among their freeborn and emancipated brethren.

As a consequence, free and non-free "colored" people had occasion to see one another and to contemplate how thin, at times, was the line that separated them. Of the 337 African Americans—although they weren't considered American citizens at the time—enumerated in the 1800 Ohio census, most were likely free, but some were undoubtedly runaways. A number of them settled among and intermarried with friendly Native Americans such as the Wyandot tribe in Upper Sandusky.

Others were workers who had previously been enslaved. They were brought to Ohio by their Southern "masters" who needed their labor to develop their land. While some may have been emancipated outright, others were required to purchase their freedom through an agreement of indenture. During the colonial era, about half of the immigrants from Europe came as indentured servants. And those who broke their indenture by running away were subject to being hunted down the same as if they were escapees from slavery or—more euphemistically—fugitives from labor or service.

Although great fortunes were built on the backs of enslaved persons, the deleterious effect of the practice was obvious to many. As early as 1812, a Scottish mapmaker, John Mellish, observed the difference between the settlers on the western side of the Ohio River and those on the eastern. Those on the Ohio side "were by far in the most comfortable circumstances."[18] On the [West] Virginia side, however, "they seemed generally to trust to the exertions of the negroes, and we found them… miserable and wretched, and poor, and almost naked."[19] Mellish attributed the condition of the white settlers to the "bad effects of slavery."[20] Twenty years later, French historian and political scientist Alexis de Tocqueville reached much the same conclusion: "In general the colony that had no slaves was more populous and prosperous than the one where slavery was

The United States accounted for less than 4 percent of the Atlantic slave trade. *Library of Congress.*

in force."[21] But few believed it then, and some defenders of slavery still doubt it today.

From the beginning, there were people who tried to circumvent the Northwest Territory's ban on slavery. Nathaniel Massie may have been one of them. Massie left his boot prints all over early Ohio. A pioneering surveyor, he is credited with laying out fourteen Ohio towns, including Chillicothe, the state's first capital. In the process, he became one of the state's largest landowners and earliest politicians.

Originally from Virginia, Massie ostensibly freed all of those he held in bondage when he left his farm in Kentucky to come to Ohio. But it may not have been the magnanimous gesture it seemed. For on May 4, 1801, Charles Willing Byrd, Massie's brother-in-law, wrote to him that an indentured servant named Abraham had turned up in Cincinnati "in pursuit of his freedom."[22] Abraham claimed that Massie had threatened "to sell him if he did not sign the indenture."[23] He was insisting, therefore, that he be emancipated—in other words, released from slavery—by the court on the grounds that his indentureship had not been a voluntary act.

Byrd's first thought was to lock Abraham up. But by the time Byrd became aware of him, the Black man had already been hired out to others. After working for at least three different employers, he was finally consigned to the Hamilton County jail. By then, Abraham had earned enough money that

Byrd had him pay for his own keep, rather than billing Massie for the cost of his servant's incarceration.

A month later, Byrd wrote another letter to Massie. He had decided to release Abraham from confinement once he "discovered symptoms of repentance."[24] Abraham was delivered back to Ross County, where he likely occupied one of the row of dwellings Massie had erected for his servants behind his own home. It probably differed little from the slave cabin he had previously occupied in Kentucky.

Thomas Worthington—"Father of Ohio Statehood" and future governor of the state—did something similar with his former slaves, promising to give them land in exchange for their help getting him established in Ohio. In short, they did, but he didn't.[25]

Because the state of Ohio was to be carved out of the Northwest Territory, congressional approval was required to begin the formal process. After it was obtained, a constitutional convention was called to order in November 1802. Thirty-five elected delegates met in Chillicothe to draft the first Ohio Constitution. Men such as Edward Tiffin, Nathaniel Massie, Thomas Worthington, Samuel Huntington, Ephraim Cutler and Rufus Putnam agreed, among other things, to prohibit slavery in Ohio in keeping with the provisions of the Northwest Ordinance of 1787.

Article VIII, section 2, of the Ohio Constitution of 1803, established:

> *There shall be neither slavery nor involuntary servitude in this State, otherwise than for the punishment of crimes, whereof the party shall have been duly convicted; nor shall any male person, arrived at the age of twenty-one years, or female person arrived at the age of eighteen years, be held to serve any person as a servant, under the pretense of indenture or otherwise, unless such person shall enter into such indenture while in a state of perfect freedom, and on a condition of a bona fide consideration, received or to be received, for their service, except as before excepted. Nor shall any indenture of any negro or mulatto, hereafter made and executed out of the State, or if made in the State, where the term of service exceeds one year, be of the least validity, except those given in the case of apprenticeships.*

This meant that people of color, including American Indians, would lead a twilight existence in which they were free but were not and could not become citizens of the State of Ohio.[26]

On January 5, 1804, the line between free and non-free African Americans became thinner when the Ohio General Assembly became the

Buckeye Station was Nathaniel Massie's first home in the Ohio Territory. *Library of Congress.*

first legislative body in the nation to enact so-called Black Laws or Black Codes. Indiana, Illinois and the Michigan Territory would soon follow. The laws were designed to restrict the rights of free Black people and discourage them from migrating to the Buckeye State.

All Black and biracial individuals were compelled to obtain a certificate of freedom from a U.S. court before they could settle in Ohio. Without this document, it was illegal for anyone to hire them. Moreover, they were required to register themselves and their children at a fee of $0.12 each. The Black Laws also made it a crime to harbor or help a fugitive slave. The offender was subjected to a fine of $1,000, half of which was paid to the informant.

Pressure to create the Black Laws came from several factions: those Ohioans who had migrated from Southern states and remained supportive of the institution of slavery; those who had strong business ties to the South and did not want to jeopardize them; and those who viewed free Black people as an economic and social threat and were afraid the state would be inundated by them. To these individuals—and their numbers were substantial—Black people had no place in Ohio, free or not. Even those who opposed slavery did not necessarily accept people of color as equals.

Before moving to Dayton, Colonel Robert Patterson had helped found the cities of Lexington, Kentucky, and Cincinnati. While his opposition to slavery influenced his decision to leave the South, Patterson, like Massie, brought a handful of enslaved workers, perhaps half a dozen, along with him to Ohio to help him get settled. He knew it was against the law, but he was clearly conflicted over how best to balance their interests against his own.

Slave owners were accustomed to having an abundance of labor available to do their bidding. In Ohio, however, labor was a scarce commodity—as scarce as the cash workers demanded in payment. By law, Patterson could bring his slaves to Ohio for unspecified periods of time "so long as they did no useful work."[27] But he could also hire free Black and "mulatto" workers through the process of indenture, if they were agreeable.

The last two enslaved persons Patterson brought to Ohio were Edward "Ned" Page and his wife, Lucy. Patterson knew that he would have to keep a close watch on the couple because they had made no secret of their desire for freedom. To circumvent the law, Patterson conspired with a friend, Dr. Andrew McCalla, to create a phony bill of sale. This way Patterson could always claim that Ned and Lucy were runaways he was holding for a friend should they subsequently cause him problems.

At the time, the settlement of Dayton consisted of fewer than twenty cabins. But despite the presence of many Southern transplants, the Pages were valued members of the community. It wasn't long before some of Patterson's neighbors encouraged the enslaved couple to petition the court for their emancipation, arguing that they were being held to labor against their will. When the case was heard by a local magistrate, the Pages were granted their freedom.

"The objections of Dayton residents," historian Emil Pocock wrote, "probably convinced McCalla that it was no longer prudent to leave his slaves in Dayton, and he soon made arrangements to bring them back to Kentucky."[28] The matter finally came to a head on January 30, 1806, when McCalla entered Newcom's Tavern. He was accompanied by David Sharp, a professional slave catcher. His intent was to arrest Ned and Lucy Page and transport them back to Kentucky with him.

The Fugitive Slave Law authorized McCalla to take the Pages before a magistrate. But knowing he would not receive a favorable ruling in Dayton, he planned to take the couple to Chillicothe instead. When Ned refused to go with him, a number of townspeople intervened. Waving a pistol that someone had likely slipped to him, Ned paced around the tavern, warning everyone he would defend himself.

Although he was also armed, Sharp announced that he was leaving. But several men—three of whom were magistrates—made it clear that they intended to stop him. Sharp then tried to make the case for arresting the Pages on the grounds that McCalla held title to them. However, Patterson had inadvertently undercut that argument by "asserting in writing that the Pages were McCalla's slaves when he made the indentures before leaving Kentucky."[29] Per Ohio law, indentureships could only be entered into with free persons.

Consequently, the magistrates declared "that Sharp was under arrest for breach of peace and would be immediately bound over for trial."[30] Exposed as a hypocrite, Patterson, along with another man, pledged $500 each as security for Sharp's appearance at the April session of the Supreme Court. Sharp and McCalla then returned to Kentucky empty-handed.

Additional and even more onerous Black Laws were passed by the Ohio General Assembly on January 25, 1807. Among other things, free Black residents were now required to not only prove they were not slaves but also find at least two people who would guarantee a bond of $500 ensuring their good behavior. And woe be it to any Black person who could not prove that he or she was freeborn or manumitted. If the matter went to court, they were forbidden to testify on their own behalf, even when their very freedom was a stake.

A clash between a slave catcher and his quarry took place in Newcom's Tavern. *Library of Congress.*

In his State of the Union address on December 2, 1806, President Thomas Jefferson called for the passage of an act prohibiting the importation of slaves into the United States. It was not a new idea. He had been advocating for it since the 1770s. And it wasn't particularly bold, since all states, following Virginia's lead, had already enacted statutes banning or restricting the international slave trade. However, South Carolina had reversed course, and the smuggling of slaves had continued more or less unabated.

As a concession to the South, the delegates to the Constitutional Convention of 1787 had agreed that they could not undertake to ban the slave trade for twenty years. When the time limit expired, Jefferson quickly moved forward with an act to prohibit any additional slaves from being brought into the United States. It went into effect on January 1, 1808, the earliest date permitted by the Constitution.

Despite this erosion of Black rights stemming from the Black Laws, Ohio came to be viewed as the "Promised Land" by many slaves. According to historian Wilbur Siebert, Ohio had the most extensive Underground Railroad network of any state. There were two reasons for this. First, it shared 400 miles of border with two slave states—Virginia, including what would become West Virginia, and Kentucky. And second, it was at most only 250 miles from Canada. Siebert estimated there were 3,000 miles of routes with more than twenty points of entry on the Ohio River.

Perhaps as early as the 1780s, fugitives from slavery were being helped by the Quakers, many of whom had moved to Ohio specifically to assist those escaping to freedom. However, the only real protection was the distance that separated the pursued from the pursuers. The farther north the slaves were able to flee, the lesser the likelihood they would be recaptured. Nevertheless, an estimated one hundred African American settlements were established in Ohio in the years leading up to the Civil War—more than in any other state.[31] And the slave hunters took notice.

Mention of the first fugitive slave case in Ohio was found among the papers of Samuel Huntington, governor of the state from 1808 to 1810. This led historian William Smith to dig through the records of Virginia to uncover additional details of the life of a Black woman known only as Jane. His account begins with a trial in Charlestown (now Wellsburg, West) Virginia, on October 22, 1808.

Jane, who was owned by Joseph Tomlinson Jr., had been charged with entering a local store under cover of darkness and stealing four dollars' worth of merchandise. That she was found guilty was not surprising, but the sentence handed down by Judge James Griffith was, at least by today's

Twelve of the first eighteen American presidents, including Thomas Jefferson, owned slaves. *Library of Congress.*

standards. He ordered that she be "confined until the tenth day of December next, and that on that day she be taken by the sheriff from the jail to the place of execution, and there, at twelve o'clock on that day, be hanged by the neck until she be dead."[32]

When the papers were received by William Cabell, Virginia's outgoing governor, on November 4, 1808, he decided that justice would be better served by issuing a reprieve until November 1, 1809, at which time she would be sold. John Connell, clerk of courts, was directed to dispose of her for the best price he could obtain and ensure she was transported out of the United States. The court set Jane's monetary value at $350.[33]

Jane had been the "beneficiary" of an act passed in 1801, which gave the governor the option to contract for the sale or purchase of slaves under sentence of death, providing they did not remain in Virginia. But before the governor was able to save her, a sympathetic jailer left the jail door open and Jane walked away. For two days, Jane lingered in Charlestown before crossing the Ohio River to Marietta. She then obtained employment as a domestic in the family of Abner Lord. In time, Jane married a free Black man and gave birth to a child.

By the laws of Ohio and the nation, Jane's owner was entitled to reclaim her. Late in 1809, Samuel Beeson came to Marietta and tried to return her to Virginia by force. When she refused to go with him, he petitioned John Tyler, Virginia's governor and future president of the United States, to assist him. Tyler sent a letter to Governor Samuel Huntington of Ohio, informing him that the justice of the peace and other residents of Marietta refused to surrender her.

Huntington replied that he could not intervene because the Fugitive Slave Law of 1793 prohibited a state executive from doing so. But he finally acquiesced when notified that Jane was not just a fugitive slave but a criminal convicted of theft. Consequently, Jane was arrested on May 21, 1810, and remanded to Beeson's custody. When she arrived back in Virginia, Governor Tyler pardoned her for her crime, but then ordered Beeson to sell her and remit the money to the state treasury. "And in June, 1810, Jane and her child disappeared in the Cimmerian darkness of slavery."[34]

Black settlements began to appear in Ohio from its earliest days. *Authors' collection.*

Given the choice, most kidnappers would probably prefer to abduct a child than an adult. The risks were certainly fewer, although the recompense might be less. In 1819, William Bell did just that, stealing a nine-year-old Black girl named Venus. It didn't matter than she wasn't a slave. Bell's plan was to take her to Fleming County, Kentucky, and sell her.

As soon as he heard about the kidnapping, Governor Ethan Allen Brown of Ohio took action. "The requisition of the Governor of Ohio for the arrest of Bell was promptly acted on by the Governor of Kentucky, who caused the miscreant to be arrested, and lodged in jail and finally delivered to the agent of the former State."[35]

While acknowledging the cooperation he received from Kentucky governor Gabriel Slaughter, Brown wrote that

> *the citizens of Kentucky should not complain that those of Ohio should feel an interest in requiring proof of ownership however inconvenient to the proprietors, before they consent to the removal of negroes against their will. The want of such evidence and the violence of attempting to remove them without the warrant of the constituted authority, I suspect, have been the chief causes of the difficulty which actual proprietors*

*have experienced in reclaiming their slaves in Ohio; and the villainy of unprincipled kidnappers has aroused the people in some districts into a vigilance which I hope you will think laudable, to guard against the perpetrators of so dark a crime.*[36]

In truth, Kentucky's citizens were not all of the same mind when it came to slavery. As Abraham Lincoln confided to a friend during his first year of office, "I think to lose Kentucky is nearly the same as to lose the whole game."[37] While the Commonwealth endeavored to remain neutral during the Civil War, some 35,000 Kentuckians served in the Confederate army and 125,000 in the Union. But years before the armies took the field, frequent skirmishes broke out along the Ohio River between pro- and antislavery advocates.

## 2

# THE LORDS OF OUR LAND

*The lords of our land to this hunting have gone,*
*As the fox-hunter follows the sound of the horn.*

—*John Greenleaf Whittier, "The Hunters of Men"*

No legislative body is better at kicking the can down the road than the United States Congress. If it doesn't want to deal with a problem, it won't. The Sixteenth Congress, which convened in 1819, struggled to come to grips with some of the same issues that had confounded the previous fifteen, not the least of which was slavery. As the country was expanding and states were calving off from the western frontier, the question to be answered in each instance was whether they would be slave or free.

The Missouri Compromise was the name given to a piece of legislation that orchestrated the admission of Maine and Missouri to the Union. Signed into law by President James Monroe on March 6, 1820, it preserved the balance of power in the U.S. Senate by stipulating that Maine would be a free state and Missouri a slave one. Henry Clay, a U.S. senator and slaveholder from Kentucky, was the principal architect, earning him the nickname "The Great Compromiser."[38]

The compromise drew a line in the sand or, rather, soil. Free soil: except for Missouri, slavery was prohibited in the western territories north of the 36°30' parallel. This was roughly the southern border of Virginia and Kentucky and the northernmost border of Texas. But it was controversial

*Above*: Senator Henry Clay from Kentucky negotiated the Missouri Compromise. *Library of Congress.*

*Right*: During his life, President James Monroe enslaved as many as 250 individuals. *Library of Congress.*

from the beginning. There were fears that a battle line was being drawn between the North and the South based on sectional differences over slavery. And they were right. Tensions would build over the next forty years.

While the Ohio Supreme Court dealt with a handful of early cases involving slaves, its decisions weren't published until 1823, and in many instances the only mention of them—if any—is in contemporary newspaper articles. That was the situation with *State v. Carneal* in 1817.

There is a lot of misinformation circulating about Thomas D. Carneal. Although he was one of Covington, Kentucky's founding fathers, he apparently did not build the first brick house in the city—the so-called Carneal house. Neither is there any evidence that he harbored fugitive slaves there. In fact, he had no known connection to the impressive mansion, and harboring fugitive slaves would appear to have been out of keeping with his character.

Carneal was a plantation owner, as well as a dealer in military supplies and, later, a state representative and banker. His wife was Sally Howell Stanley. She was the widowed sister of the first wife of Nicholas Longworth, a wealthy Cincinnati businessman and Carneal's sometimes business partner. Given the extent of his landholdings, it is not surprising that Carneal owned slaves. He also hired out some of them to work across the river in Ohio. When this was discovered, he was charged with holding one man in particular, Richard Lunsford, in bondage.

"At the trial Lunsford proved that he had lived on and off in Ohio and had been hired out there," historian Paul Finkelman wrote.[39] In fact, he had apparently been "sold" (in other words, leased) to a James Riddle, who worked him in Ohio for eight to ten days at a time.

In delivering his opinion, Judge John McLean made it clear that he had no use for slavery:

> *Were it proper to consider it, the Court, as well as from the principles recognized by our Constitution and Laws, could not hesitate in declaring that SLAVERY* [emphasis in original], *except for the punishment of crimes, is an infringement upon the sacred rights of man: Rights, which he derives from his Creator, and which are inalienable.*[40]

Nevertheless, McLean believed that under the U.S. Constitution, which he was sworn to uphold, he had no choice but to respect the property rights of citizens from other states. Nevertheless, he then freed Lunsford after discovering a loophole in Carneal's legal title to him.

On the court, John McLean was an important opponent of slavery. *Library of Congress.*

Not all loopholes, however, were in the slave's favor. In March 1808, a Black woman, Milly, along with her husband, Naise, applied for a writ of habeas corpus in Gallia County. They were seeking to obtain their freedom from John Rodgers, who claimed them as his slaves. Evidently, they had been brought to Ohio from Virginia to perform work for him in southern Ohio. They won—or so it seemed. The judgment of the court was to "go hence, be discharged, and set at liberty."[41]

A day later, Rodgers approached Edward Tupper and asked him to persuade Milly to live with him for two years. If she agreed, then he would execute "a complete deed of manumission, which should put the question of her liberty at rest," rather than risk having another court reverse the judgment.[42] Both Milly and Naise agreed, providing Rodgers made out the manumission papers in advance. The deed of absolute manumission was subsequently "executed in Gallia county, Ohio, on the 2d April, 1808, John Rodgers styling himself in it, a citizen of Virginia."[43]

Milly and Naise returned to Virginia with Rodgers, where she later gave birth to a son, Lewis. There is reason to believe that Milly upheld her end of the bargain, but her husband likely didn't. As a result, neither one of them may have been freed. Whatever the case, Rodgers maintained custody of Lewis. Then in 1821, Milly brought suit on behalf of Lewis in Cabell County, [West] Virginia, against William Fullerton and Jane Rodgers—John Rodgers's heirs—in an effort to obtain her son's freedom. The question was whether a contract made in Ohio to be executed in Virginia was legally governed by the laws of Ohio or Virginia.

In delivering the opinion of the court in *Lewis v. Fullerton*, Judge Roan noted that the appellant—Lewis—claimed he had a right to freedom on the grounds that his mother had acquired her freedom in Ohio prior to his birth. But Roan contended that there was no evidence of Milly having been a resident of Ohio per se. Rather, her presence there was merely transitory, and a slave removing from Virginia to Ohio with the master's consent for a mere transitory purpose "does not thereby acquire a right to freedom in Virginia."[44]

Roan rejected the argument that Milly was free simply because a witness had seen her working at a sugar camp in Ohio outside the presence of her master. Furthermore, a "judgment of *habeas corpus* in Ohio, in favor of the slave, does not establish his right to freedom."[45] Finally, a deed of emancipation executed in Ohio is void unless it is recorded in the requisite country court of Virginia—which it had not been.

A number of slaveholders held title to their relatives. Miscegenation—the interbreeding of different races—was the dirty little secret underpinning many of these "special" relationships between master and slave. However, it would be a mistake to romanticize them as love stories, given the difference in the power dynamic. They were anything but consensual.

Kate Daily was a slave belonging to a Miss Baker of Mason County, Kentucky. She later married Alexander Edwards. When her husband subsequently passed away in 1823, a sale of his property was held. At that time, Kate was purchased by her brother, Thomas Daily, for $161. No one else bid on the enslaved woman because Thomas had stated his intention to emancipate her, which he did on January 12, 1824. As it was later revealed, no provision had been made for Kate's welfare after she was freed. However, James Dummitt, who had purchased four of her children at the sale, invited her to move to his plantation, where he built a cabin for her so that she could raise them. There she gave birth to a son, Tom.

In April 1828, Thomas Daily contracted to buy a slave from Joseph Desha, the governor of Kentucky.[46] Because he did not have enough money to cover the full purchase price, Thomas gave Desha a bill of sale on his sister's son, Tom. The bill of sale would be voided if Thomas paid Desha the money he owed him by October 7, 1829. But Desha grew anxious and threatened to seize the boy and place him in slavery.

Somehow, Kate learned that Tom's freedom was in jeopardy, so she sent him to Cincinnati to stay with a friend, Orange Witt. Governor Desha immediately appealed to the mayor of Cincinnati, who had Tom arrested and held for a hearing. According to historian Leo Alilunas, "The argument was presented in court that Desha knew that Kate was free before the birth of Tom, even though no deed of emancipation has been made."[47] But Desha insisted he didn't and, to the contrary, had been told by Thomas Daily that he never planned to give his sister her freedom and that she was not freed until six months after the boy was born.

For his part, Thomas Daily was noncommittal on whether the youth was freeborn. But he did reveal that he had conspired with Desha and Dummitt to keep the whole scheme a secret from Kate. Nevertheless, he was still planning to pay Desha the money he owed him—$120—prior to it becoming due.

In the end, the Ohio Supreme Court ruled in the case of *Tom v. Daily* that Kate was free five months before Tom's birth, and therefore, Tom was free, too. Neither Thomas Daily nor Governor Desha had any claim on him. In its decision, the court asserted:

> *It is a well-settled rule that no man shall take advantage of his own wrong. The conduct of Daily at the administrator's sale was a fraud. By his declarations and promises he was enabled to purchase his sister at less than half value; and that, too, by imposing on the humanity of the by-standers.*

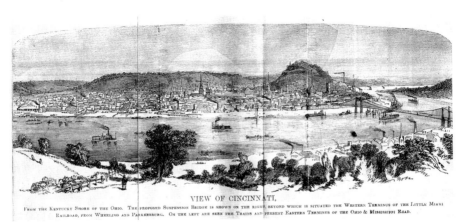

VIEW OF CINCINNATI,

FROM THE KENTUCKY SHORE OF THE OHIO. THE PROPOSED SUSPENSION BRIDGE IS SHOWN ON THE RIGHT, BEYOND WHICH IS SITUATED THE WESTERN TERMINUS OF THE LITTLE MIAMI RAILROAD, FROM WHEELING AND PARKERSBURG. ON THE LEFT ARE SEEN THE TRAINS AND PRESENT EASTERN TERMINUS OF THE OHIO & MISSISSIPPI ROAD.

Situated on the Ohio River, Cincinnati was an important gateway to freedom. *Authors' collection.*

*Will a court of equity now permit him to turn round and claim his sister and her offspring as slaves?*[48]

Daily's behavior calls into question whether Kate was actually his sister or half sister. In 1830, there were African American slaveholders found in twenty-nine Kentucky counties. Obviously, it was possible for a free Black man to buy slaves. However, Ohio's Black Laws prohibited Black people from testifying in court—this included the Supreme Court of Ohio. Therefore, Thomas Daily must have been white and Kate the biracial product of a sexual relationship with Thomas's father.

Cincinnati was a microcosm of the political divisions that rent the country. As historian Henry Howe described it:

> *The three elements of population, and we might say of civilization, northern, central, and southern, met together on the shores of the Ohio, and Cincinnati became a cauldron of boiling opinions, a crucible of ignited ideas. There was a time when Southern alkali seemed to prevail over Northern oxide, and the aristocratic young city was dominated by cavalier sentiment. Cincinnati, by the accident of geographical position, became the focus of Abolitionism, and also of the opposite sentiment.*[49]

The "opposite sentiment" was put on display in what is known as the Cincinnati Riots of 1829.[50]

Shortly after the Ohio Supreme Court upheld the constitutionality of the state's Black Laws, the free people of color in Cincinnati were given notice on June 30, 1829, that they had thirty days to post surety bonds of $500 or they would be expelled from the city. Charles Hammond, editor of the *Cincinnati Daily Gazette*, no doubt believed it when he wrote: "That part of our coloured population who are free, who are honest, who are industrious and correct in their deportment have nothing to fear from the enforcement of the laws. It is only the runaway slaves and idle vagrants that have occasion for alarm."[51]

Pressure to do something about the growing Black population in Cincinnati—the largest of any city in the Old Northwest—had been building. It was reflected in the results of the recent election in which a major issue was how to limit the number of "Negroes." The city's African American residents knew that any such action posed a threat to them all. The *Cincinnati Emporium* reported that two thousand of them had chosen delegates to arrange for their removal, asking only that they be granted three months to do so. The newspaper felt that was a reasonable request. The delegates had begun negotiations to purchase "the Gulf of Blue Lands" in Canada, where there were already two settlements, one Dutch and the other Quaker.[52] But not everyone was willing to wait for this arrangement to be completed.

Between August 15 and August 22, 1829, there was a series of violent clashes as mobs of white citizens entered the Black neighborhoods of the First Ward, intent on driving the residents out of Cincinnati. Many were killed or wounded, much property was destroyed and, in the end, an estimated 1,200 to 2,000 people of color left the city—although historian Nikki Taylor argues that for a portion of that number it "should not be considered an act of mass victimization," but of "self-determination," because some of them were already planning to leave.[53]

One thing slaveholders everywhere feared was the possibility that their bondsmen might take up arms against them. As early as 1739, twenty slaves led by a man named Jemmy staged a revolt at Stono River in South Carolina. As they marched toward St. Augustine, Florida, where they hoped to gain their freedom under Spanish law, their ranks swelled to one hundred or so. For a week, they fought with the English colonists before they were finally defeated. It was the first revolt, but it would not be the last.

In terms of audacity, body count and widespread panic, Nat Turner's Rebellion was unrivaled as far as slave insurrections in the United States are concerned. Driven by voices and visions from "God," Turner and his compatriots killed fifty-five to sixty-five people in Southampton County, Virginia, during August 1831. But the uprising was crushed within three days.

Following Turner's revolt, legislatures in the South took measures to increase the cruelty of their slave codes. Meanwhile, a grassroots movement had come into existence to aid runaway slaves in their flight for freedom. Over time it would come be called the Underground Railroad.

Freedom in Ohio was pretty much a crapshoot for fugitive slaves. It depended largely on local politics—very local. Which justice, which commissioner, which day. And people of color were banned from participating on their own behalf, so the odds favored the house—the plantation house, that is. In Matilda Lawrence's case, this was the one downriver.

Matilda was an attractive young brunette, age twenty or so. According to William Birney, Matilda's father and owner was Larkin Lawrence, a wealthy planter from Missouri. He was also elderly, unmarried and an invalid. In 1836, Lawrence decided to spend the winter in New York in order to consult with the most eminent doctors concerning his health. Requiring Matilda's services, he took her along with him as his daughter.

An "octoroon," Matilda "gave no suspicion of the fatal taint in her blood," Birney wrote.[54] But her parentage was common knowledge back home. As a result, she was not accepted into white society, and her father forbade her association with Black society. Caught between two worlds, hers was a lonely existence indeed.

While in New York, Matilda learned about the rights of free Black people in the North and also got a taste of what it was like to pass for white. As a result, "she begged [her father] not to be taken back to Missouri and the isolation of plantation life, with the dreary prospect of the auction block at her father's death."[55] But he wouldn't hear of it. Then in May 1836, they started home.

When they reached Cincinnati, Lawrence booked them into a hotel near the wharf and purchased tickets for the next steamboat to St. Louis. Matilda pleaded with him to provide her with manumission papers, promising that she would then return to Missouri and serve him faithfully. But he refused, and she seized the opportunity to sneak out of the hotel. Matilda made her way to a barbershop operated by a Black man who concealed her in his home for several days. By then, her father had departed for St. Louis, but had hired agents to be on the lookout for her.

Matilda soon found employment with a white family. Then in October, she was hired by Agatha Birney as a nurse and chambermaid. Her husband, James G. Birney, was the publisher of *The Philanthropist*, an abolitionist newspaper. Their son William wrote that everyone in his family thought the young woman was white. She revealed little of her history to them, other than that she had been born in Missouri, her mother was dead and she did not want to live with her father.

Early in March 1837, Matilda returned from an errand, "pale and trembling with fright, and begged [Agatha Birney] to save her from being seized as a slave."[56] She had been confronted by a man she did not know who accused her of being a fugitive. Matilda then spilled out the details of her story. When James Birney learned what had happened, he advised the young woman to go into hiding until they could send her to one of their friends in western New York.

However, the Birney home was under constant surveillance by John W. Riley, "a notorious negro hunter and kidnapper."[57] And on March 10, 1857, Matilda was taken into custody on a warrant issued by Justice William Doty of Hamilton County with no proof other than an affidavit submitted by Riley. In fact, the Birneys doubted that Lawrence was involved at all. Nevertheless, they surrendered the young woman to the authorities and

Abolitionist James G. Birney
was an inspiration and
mentor to many others.
*Library of Congress.*

hired attorney Salmon P. Chase to defend her. Politically a Whig, Chase, under Birney's mentorship, would later receive the nickname "the attorney general for escaped slaves."[58]

"Mr. Chase argued, upon an application for a writ of *habeas corpus*, that when a slave-owner voluntarily brought his slave into a free State, the slave by that act became free, and could in no sense be termed a fugitive, or be reclaimed under the Fugitive Slave Law of 1793."[59] But Chase lost the case, as he almost always would, and Matilda was remanded to Riley.

"As soon as it was pronounced by the judge, the young girl, sobbing in her terror, was seized by three stout hired ruffians, hurried through the crowd, placed in a carriage in waiting, driven rapidly to the wharf, and taken by ferryboat to Covington, where she was put in jail for safe keeping."[60] Later than night, Matilda was placed on a steamboat to New Orleans. Sold at public auction, she immediately vanished from the pages of history.

That should have been the end of it, except that Birney was then charged with harboring a fugitive slave. Once again, Chase offered a valiant defense, but with a similar result. "The accused spoke about three hours in his own defense, admitting the facts, and maintaining that Matilda Lawrence was in law a free woman," William Birney related. "His argument made many converts, especially among the younger members of the bar."[61] But the jury didn't care for his antislavery politics. They found him guilty, and he was sentenced to pay fifty dollars and court costs.

As Chase was leaving the courtroom, he overheard one of the spectators say of him, "There is a promising young man, who has just ruined himself."[62] However, when he appealed the case to the Ohio Supreme Court in *Birney v. Ohio*, Chase won an unaccustomed victory. But it was not on the strength of his argument. "Chase purposely omitted to call attention to the fact that the indictment contained no averment that the defendant knew the person harbored to be a slave, preferring to renew his former contention," according to a court historian, "for if Matilda were not a slave, Mr. Birney could not be guilty of harboring her as a fugitive."[63]

The justices asserted that since Ohio was a free state, the girl's skin color alone was not enough for Birney to assume that she was a slave. As Justice Reuben Wood wrote, "[T]he presumption is in favor of freedom.…[I]t cannot be assumed that an act which…involves no moral wrong, nay, an act that in many cases would be highly praiseworthy, should be made grievously criminal, when performed in total unconsciousness of the facts that infect it with crime."[64]

The Supreme Court also "requested that Chase's arguments be published, although at the time the court had a rule prohibiting publication of arguments of the counsel except at the court's discretion. This indicated that the court was interested in giving publicity to the legality of the issue."[65]

# 3

# THOUGH HUNDREDS ARE CAUGHT

*All blithe are our hunters, and noble their match,*
*Though hundreds are caught, there are millions to catch.*
*—John Greenleaf Whittier, "The Hunters of Men"*

Although British merchants were heavily invested in the Atlantic slave trade, Britain was also a leader in the movement to abolish slavery, beginning with the Slave Trade Act of 1807. But it wasn't until a quarter of a century later that Parliament passed an act to do away with slavery in most British colonies—excepting the islands of Ceylon and Saint Helena, and any territories in possession of the East India Company. This act took effect on August 1, 1834. Yet only slaves under the age of six were actually freed. Those six and above were made apprentices and had to complete a period of servitude.

By then, the Northern states had all taken steps to eliminate slavery, although it was a gradual process that did not immediately grant all enslaved persons their freedom. In fact, it is estimated that more than one million slaves from the North were subsequently sold to the Deep South. Meanwhile, the Southern states clung to the institution of slavery—and, more importantly, the lifestyle it afforded—and showed little inclination to give it up.

During the antebellum period, the Northern states held the majority in the House of Representatives from the time of the first congress. In the Senate, there was essentially an equal division between the North and the South, save for a three-year period during which the Southern states held a majority. After 1850, however, the South would become a permanent minority. And they saw it coming.

On the other hand, the South had a stranglehold on the executive and judicial branches of government prior to the Civil War. "Thirteen of the first 16 presidential elections were won by Southerners, and the two subsequent winners (Franklin Pierce and James Buchanan) were famously 'Northern men of Southern principles,'" according to historian J. Gordon Hylton.[66] In addition, nineteen of thirty-three justices who served on the U.S. Supreme Court were from Southern states.

As enmity continued to build between the free states and the slave, Congress attempted to deescalate the situation by refusing to discuss it. In May 1836, the House of Representatives passed a "gag rule" automatically postponing action on all bills or petitions related to slavery. John Quincy Adams, who, like his father, had never owned slaves, tried to rally opposition to it, but the timing wasn't right. There could be no civil discourse without civil discord. The United States, just sixty years old, was being pulled apart.

Elisha Brazealle fathered John Monroe Brazealle by one of his slaves. According to Mississippi law, John was a slave, too, although half white. But in 1826, after Elisha fell ill and was "nursed back to health by his mulatta slave," he took the boy and the boy's mother to Ohio, emancipated them and married her.[67] Afterward, they returned to Jefferson County, Mississippi. Clearly, the slaveholder was trying to bestow a degree of normalcy on their relationship, although interracial marriages were banned in Mississippi.

Taking it one step farther, Elisha bequeathed to his son the proceeds from his estate. Not surprisingly, the Hinds family—who considered themselves the rightful heirs—challenged the bequest. In the case of *Hinds v. Brazealle*, the High Court of Errors and Appeals at Natchez set the provisions of the will aside.[68] John and his mother, in the court's view, were still slaves.

As Chief Justice William Sharkey wrote in 1838:

> *The state of the case shews conclusively, that this contract had its origin in an offense against morality, pernicious and detestable as an example; but above all, it seems to have been planned and executed with a fixed design to evade the rigor of the laws of this State. The acts of the party, in going to Ohio with the slaves, and there executing the deed, and his immediate return with them to this State, point with unerring certainty to his purpose and object. The laws of this State cannot be thus defrauded of their operation by one of our own citizens.*[69]

Although there were slave markets throughout the South, few traces of them remain. *Authors' collection.*

Author Harriet Beecher Stowe would base the character of Cora Gordon in her 1856 novel *Dred: A Tale of the Great Dismal Swamp* on the unidentified woman in the Brazealle case. It was, in part, a response to criticism of her earlier novel *Uncle Tom's Cabin*, because Tom was seen as too passive by some Black people and abolitionists.

In the fall of 1838, "Black Bill" Mitchell (aka Anderson) arrived in Marion, Ohio. His talents as a butcher, barber and laborer, not to mention fiddler, banjoist and square dance caller, quickly made him a valued member of the community. Many Marion residents were willing to overlook the possibility that he was also a fugitive from labor.

Less than a year later in July 1839, a posse of eight men from Kanawha County, Virginia, showed up. They claimed that Mitchell was a slave belonging to Adnah Van Bibber. He was promptly arrested under Ohio's fugitive slave law and placed in jail to await trial the following month.

The citizens of Marion were not happy about this development, having taken Mitchell at his word that he was a "free nigger."[70] So on Monday, August 26, 1839, when the case was heard by Judge Ozias Bowen, the courtroom was packed to the walls. Van Bibber and his men had traveled from Virginia to attend the hearing. "These slave hunters," one local historian wrote, "came fully armed with Bowie-knives and pistols which they brandished and flourished in a threatening way, to intimidate the friends of Black Bill."[71]

The myth of the "happy slave" persists to this day among apologists for slavery. *Authors' collection.*

The trial was a lopsided affair, with most of the witnesses supporting Van Bibber. Mitchell, being a person of color, was not permitted to testify in his own defense, so he was represented by Cooper K. Watson and James H. Godman. On Tuesday morning, however, Judge Bowen surprised everyone by granting the prisoner his freedom on a technicality: Van Bibber didn't own Mitchell—John Lewis, his cousin, did.

As soon as the judge made his ruling, Van Bibber and his men seized Mitchell. Waving their weapons and threatening the lives of all who tried to stop them, they dragged the Black man out of the courthouse and through the streets of Marion. "At this unusual and horrible sight, the populace became enraged, and attacked them with stones, and whatever missiles they could get hold of," another historian related.[72] Followed down the street by an angry mob, the Virginians took shelter in the offices of Judge John Bartram. Van Bibber argued for a new trial while the masses outside demanded he surrender Mitchell to them.

When the sheriff arrived at the scene, he begged the crowd to disperse, but they refused. Instead, someone called for them to break into the arsenal to obtain weapons, which they did. Now, both sides were armed to the teeth. Finally, Judge Anderson, ignoring the knives and the pistols, forced his way into Bartram's office. Others followed, breaking through a rear door and allowing Mitchell to escape. When one of the Virginians gave chase and threatened to shoot him, the throng immediately jumped the man, knocking him and one of his accomplices to the ground.

Eventually, the Virginians were all placed under arrest. But Mitchell could not be found, having fled for his life. The first night he spent in a swamp before making his way to the house of Reuben Benedict, a Quaker. He was then passed along to a Quaker settlement in Fredericktown, another in Huron County, then the town of Oberlin, before receiving an escort to Canada.

Meanwhile, Van Bibber and his men were found guilty of contempt of court. "Although they were fined $15 and costs, the fine was dropped and they wound up paying about a total of forty cents."[73] A letter subsequently published in the *Philanthropist* stated that the Virginians were threatening to sue Mitchell's rescuers for the value of the slave.

The *Cincinnati Gazette* of May 12, 1841, reported that Mary Towns had absconded from a Kentucky plantation a decade before. Known as "Rose," she was the "living property" (to quote Harriet Beecher Stowe) of Thomas Gaither. Ten years later, Gaither successfully recaptured the woman after obtaining a warrant for her arrest from Justice R.A. Madison of Cincinnati. Although Judge Richard Ayres subsequently "denied [him] the certificate [of removal] on grounds that Gaither did not produce sufficient evidence that Towns was actually a runaway slave," he did not release the woman.[74] Instead, he gave the slaver a second opportunity to prove his case.

Local abolitionists lined up attorneys Salmon P. Chase and Flamen Ball to defend Towns. In a deposition, "Towns claimed that John W. Woodson had permitted her to come to Ohio in 1831 as a hired-out slave."[75] For a period of seven years, she worked for J.C. Tunis. She also met and married Watson Towns, a Cincinnati resident. When the case was heard by Judge Nathaniel C. Reed, he found that Gaither's affidavit did not indicate that she had escaped from Kentucky. Therefore, he released her on this technicality.

Reed had been the opposing attorney when Chase represented Matilda Lawrence and James G. Birney three years earlier. But now he seemed to side with Chase, saying, "Liberty is the rule, involuntary servitude the exception" in the free state of Ohio.[76]

On May 15, 1841, the following notice appeared in the Saturday edition of the *Cincinnati Enquirer*:

> *$50 REWARD.—Whereas, certain persons (six in number) did during our absence from the city on Wednesday last, riotously and unlawfully enter our dwelling house, situate on Sixth street, no person being therein or present but Mrs. Burnett, whose age is about fifty-four years; and then proceeded forcibly and without leave, to search said house, and did unlock all the inside doors and open the same, and broke the upper floor to examine the garret. The life of Mrs. Burnett being threatened, she eventually escaped from her house, the rioters continued in possession of the same for more than two hours. The above reward will be paid to anyone who will give information to the undersigned, so as to enable them to bring the aforesaid offenders to justice.*

> ### *CORNELIUS BURNETT, JOSEPH A. BURNETT*[77]

The Burnetts were Englishmen and well-known abolitionists. This did not make them particularly popular among their Cincinnati neighbors. However, the incident described here was rather minor compared to what would follow a month later.

Newspapers of the era were extremely partisan, especially when it came to the issue of slavery, so much so that it is often difficult to reconcile their stories and arrive at some agreement on the facts. The *Philanthropist* charged that the account in the *Enquirer* could not be attributed "to anything but a deliberate purpose to excite the passions of the people by scandalous misrepresentation" while the statement in the *Cincinnati Gazette* was "one-sided, and in essential matters incorrect."[78]

A friend of the fugitive from slavery, Salmon P. Chase helped establish the Republican Party. *Library of Congress.*

According to the *Philanthropist*, a "mulatto" went to the home of Joseph Burnett on Fifth Street near Vine on a Thursday evening. He identified himself as a slave from Kentucky whose master had given him a pass to come to Cincinnati. He remained in the house overnight.

On Friday morning, June 25, 1841, Cornelius Burnett, along with his son Joseph, Joseph's wife, an employee named Jacob Lewis and two young apprentices—M. Erickson or Nickerson and F. Leveridge—were having breakfast while their Black guest sat in the corner. Without warning, three (or possibly four) men stormed into the room through the adjoining confectionery store. Joseph demanded to know what they wanted but received no reply.

Realizing they were searching for the slave, Cornelius tried to divert their attention by crying out, "Go a-head!" and pointing outside to the yard.[79] However, one of them, John McCalla (or M'Caulley), saw the Black man still sitting in the corner and exclaimed, "That is my boy! Seize him!"[80]

Despite the Burnetts ordering them to leave, the men rushed the slave. Cornelius immediately got one of them—presumably Constable Robert

Black—in a headlock and propelled him out the door, but not before the man punched him in the face. While Joseph wrestled with McCalla, his wife, Mary Ann, tried to pull him away but was struck two or three times across the neck and shoulders with a knotted stick. McCalla, who also tore her cape, shoved her across the room.

Mary's "husband fell upon [her attacker] with redoubled vigor—was thrown down—while prostrate, McCalla drew a pistol, pointed it at his breast, pulled the trigger, but it missed fire," *The Liberator* reported.[81]

Hearing the commotion, Leveridge came running up from downstairs and grabbed McCalla. This freed Joseph to give McCalla a severe flogging and drive him out of the building. However, the enslaved man had been seized by another man in the party and hurried away. He was purportedly taken before Judge George Ayers immediately following the incident and agreed to return to bondage.

By then, the sound of the scuffle had attracted a crowd to the door of Joseph's house. Seeing McCalla's badly bleeding face, hearing that the Burnetts had been harboring runaway slaves and knowing that they were Englishmen besides, the people were greatly incensed. As the "report spread over the city—a great number of low characters, and half-grown boys, and respectable citizens, assembled about the store. Threats of violence were freely uttered."[82] In the absence of the mayor and marshal, who were away in Kentucky, Sheriff John C. Avery stepped into restore the peace. But as soon as he departed, the mob returned.

Standing in the doorway, Cornelius threatened to shoot them if they attempted to enter the building. Nevertheless, someone hurled a large stone. Picking it up, Cornelius stood outside on the pavement and held it aloft as proof of the rabble's cowardice, but this only served to anger them more. On the advice of friends, the Burnetts shuttered the windows and closed the doors, but the mob removed a shutter and broke a window. They then started to tear down the awning.

When Cornelius, stone in hand, went to the door to stop them, they knocked him down. His sons—Joseph, Thomas and Alfred, along with Lewis—hurried to his assistance, but they were knocked down as well. They had to fight their way back inside the house. All were bruised and battered, especially Thomas, and fifteen-year-old Alfred sustained a deep cut on his head. Joseph's wife was also roughed up and cursed.

That afternoon, Cornelius and his three sons, along with Leveridge, Lewis and Nickerson and another apprentice, were all arrested. They were taken before Squire Doty with a gang trailing behind. As the mob was

Fair-skinned Fannie Virginia Casseopia Lawrence was "redeemed" from slavery. *Library of Congress.*

on foot, a steamboat captain was heard to say he would give "five dollars to anyone who would drive Burnett, from Cincinnati."[83] A pork merchant said he would as well and that there was not a merchant in Cincinnati who wouldn't do the same. Along with other local businessmen, they were all complaining that business had declined since the recent rulings by the U.S.

Supreme Court. On March 9, 1841, the court ruled that in the *Amistad* slave ship mutiny—*U.S. v. The Amistad*—the Africans had been illegally forced into slavery and were, therefore, free under American law.[84]

The situation was so out of control that, during the hearing, a Mr. Bunting acknowledged that he was an antislavery man and was promptly struck in the mouth. The rabble then drove him out of the office. Some of them continued to follow him down the street and hit him several times before he sought refuge in a lawyer's office.

Although they denied any guilt, the Burnetts and their companions felt they should remain in jail as a safety precaution until the excitement had died down, so they declined to pay $3,000 in bail. As they were being conveyed to jail, the constables had to protect the abolitionists from the mob, which threatened to lynch them. However, all but Cornelius and Joseph were bailed out of jail that night. They would be convicted a month later. In court, McCalla claimed the group had a warrant for a fugitive slave's arrest. Furthermore, he said that the runaway had stolen his horse, ridden it to the river and then crossed over to Ohio. The *Cincinnati Gazette* asserted that Burnett was "oftener in troubles of a kind similar to this, than half the other abolitionists in the city together."[85]

Despite the fact that the 1829 riots had resulted in a precipitous drop in the African American population of Cincinnati, there were some who remained, and there would be others who joined them. The influx of poor, uneducated people of color, attracted by the desire for freedom and the prospect of finding work on the city's waterfront, had led to the development of Bucktown along the river. Merchants complained that the presence of this slum discouraged steamboat passengers from venturing into the city to shop. And for some white laborers, particularly the Irish immigrants, the Black workers competed directly with them for the low-skilled jobs.

In April and July 1836, there would be a similar riot pitting white against Black. Abolitionist James G. Birney, a former slave owner from Alabama, had started an abolitionist newspaper, the *Philanthropist*, in nearby New Richmond, Clermont County, Ohio. However, he then moved it to Cincinnati, despite strong opposition to his antislavery views. Soon thereafter, a mob of white, largely Irish, rioters attacked the Black residents of the lower West End, forcing them from their homes and setting fire to a tenement. Several of them died before Governor Robert Lucas declared martial law and restored order.

Three months later, another riot erupted, this time directed at Birney. Some forty men attacked his printing office, tore up his newspaper and

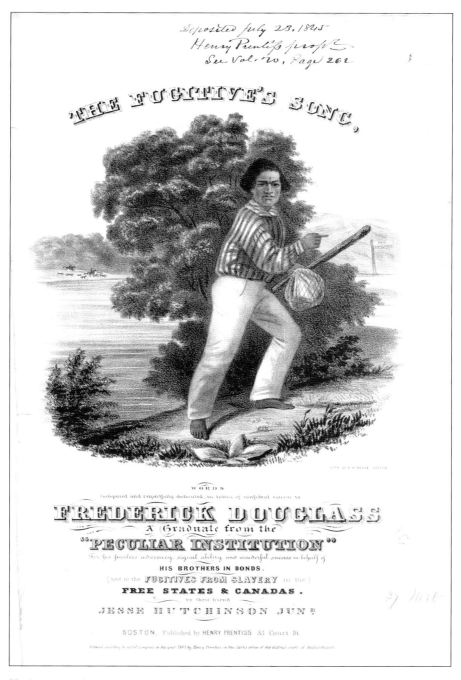

Having escaped from slavery himself, Frederick Douglass became something of a folk hero. *Library of Congress.*

destroyed his printing press. Several houses were also set ablaze in a Black neighborhood called "The Swamp." Although the riots were intended to drive out the African American residents of the city, they were also meant to be a warning to all abolitionists. However, they had the opposite effect on Attorney Salmon P. Chase, whose sister had been forced to flee from the mob. Horrified by what he witnessed, he changed sides, becoming a staunch antislavery advocate in the court system.

Nevertheless, Cincinnati continued to be a microcosm of the larger conflict that was gripping the nation. Between 1826 and 1840, the Black population had jumped from 620 to 2,240. Many white residents were in a panic that Black people were going to overrun the city, snapping up the available jobs and housing. No doubt they were incited by the many Southern sympathizers who had relocated there.

On August 1, 1841, the Black community in Cincinnati held ceremonies commemorating the Slavery Abolition Act of 1833, which abolished slavery in nearly all British colonies. Some white citizens—mostly Irish—viewed this as a provocation. During the month, tensions mounted. Finally, on the evening of August 31, there was an all-out brawl.

Other fights broke out during subsequent days. Mayor Samuel W. Davies responded by cracking down on and arresting every Black man his men could find—some three hundred altogether. As a band of Kentucky slave catchers searched the jail for fugitives, another gang of white men marched on Bucktown (or "Little Africa") in Cincinnati's third major race riot in the previous dozen years.

By this time, Cincinnati was the sixth-largest city in the country. And as a big city, it had big city problems—poverty, crime, squalor and racial turmoil. Nearly 40 percent of the population was foreign born, and 5 percent was African American. But it felt like more. It was often the first stop for those escaping slavery, and some decided not to move on.

Harriet Beecher Stowe, who was living in Cincinnati at the time, was horrified by the reports she heard from those who were fleeing the violence. John Mercer Langston, an esteemed Black educator and politician who witnessed the riot as a child, later declared it "the blackest and most detestable moment in Cincinnati's history."[86]

## 4

# SO SPEED TO THEIR HUNTING

*So speed to their hunting, o'er mountain and glen,*
*Through cane-brake and forest,—the hunting of men!*
—*John Greenleaf Whittier, "The Hunters of Men"*

According to William S. Bedford, a conductor on the Underground Railroad, a slaveholder named Bennet Raines left his home in Rockingham County, Virginia, in 1839, to go to Missouri. He departed in a hurry owing to financial difficulties of some sort. Traveling with him were his family, including Elizabeth and Eliza (presumably his wife and daughter) and four bondservants. They were Molly, Sarah, Adam and Mary—an old woman, her daughter and two children, "one four years of age and the other an infant in arms."[87] After passing through Springboro, Ohio, they camped one mile to the west near Franklin in Warren County.

"Word had been sent to the Abolitionists there of their intended arrival," Bedford recalled, "and a hope expressed that they might manage to free these slaves."[88] Bedford, along with a number of other Quakers, quickly convened a meeting. They decided to pay a visit on the Virginians to inform them that they were in violation of Ohio law by transporting slaves through the state. Dr. Abraham Brooks was designated to be the group's spokesman.

The would-be rescuers set out on November 6, 1839. As soon as they were seen approaching, however, the men in Raines's party brandished their guns and threatened violence. The abolitionists, some of whom were Black, told the men that they were in Ohio and were expected to adhere to Ohio laws. Meanwhile, the women had herded the slaves into a tent and refused to allow the Quakers and their allies to speak to them.

Raines said that the abolitionists could take any of the slaves who were willing to go, and the two women soon climbed into Bedford's carriage. "One of the children, a boy of three [or four] years of age, was found to be missing and after a long search was discovered tightly clasped in the arms of a young women…and covered closely in bed."[89] The little boy had been hidden by Raines's daughter, who may have planned to sell him when they reached Missouri. Wrested from her arms by one of the posse members, the young boy was delivered to his mother.

This upset Raines, who poked his gun barrel out of the tent or wagon where he was hiding. He was immediately greeted by the sound of ramrods and gunlocks as the abolitionists brought out their own firearms. Not more than twenty minutes later, the carriage containing all four enslaved individuals drove off, and its occupants were taken to a conductor on the Underground Railroad. Instead of going on to Canada, they settled among the Quakers.

Shortly thereafter, the Virginians arrived in the town of Franklin. They claimed that not only had their slaves been taken from them but also that they had been robbed of $500 in gold and $1,000 in paper. Since Franklin and the surrounding area was pro-slavery in its sympathies, the local citizens became riled up by the affair. The mob arrested several of the abolitionists and placed them in jail. As noted in the *Cincinnati Gazette*, Cyrus F. Farr and fifteen (or sixteen) other men, both Black and white, were ordered to appear before the court in Lebanon.

However, the "mobocrats not satisfied with this organized a band of forty men to lynch the individual most obnoxious to them, and who was accused of stealing the money."[90] Fortunately, the object of their rancor lived some twenty-two miles away, and several men who opposed the plan persuaded the others to abandon it. Still, the man and his family were forced to vacate their home each night for several weeks just to be safe.

The rescue of the four slaves was condemned by a majority of the local populace. A grand jury brought indictments against them for assault and battery, grand larceny, riot, enticing the slaves to leave their master and other offenses, including a breach of Virginia and Missouri law. The atmosphere was so charged that it was nearly impossible to seat a jury. One prospective juror when questioned expressed the opinion that "every damned abolitionist in the State should have his throat cut."[91] He was excused, but others not so open about their bias were seated.

Ostensibly, the question to be answered was, did a slaveholder have the right to take his slaves through the state of Ohio without them being granted their freedom? Raines failed to prove that the slaves were his, so the point was moot. While the prosecutor abandoned four counts of the indictment, he retained two—those pertaining to assault and battery and simple riot. As defined by Ohio law, a riot is "where three or more assemble together with intent to do an unlawful act, with force and violence, against the peace—or, if lawfully assembled, where they shall agree to do such act, and more or prepare therefor [*sic*]."[92]

As Stephen Middleton later observed, the case is unique in the history of slave rescues because it did not involve kidnapping. Nevertheless, the larger question was "very ably argued by the Prosecuting Attorney (Mr. Williams) on the part of the claimant, and Messrs. Bebb, of Hamilton, and Schenk, of Dayton, on behalf of the defendants."[93] The case was finally handed to the jury as night fell on the fourth day of the trial. They subsequently found all the defendants guilty, despite the fact that three of them had not been identified by any of the witnesses.

According to the *Cleaveland* [sic] *Palladium*, the jury misunderstood the judge's charge to them. They believed they must find three of the accused guilty of riot, but since they could not agree on which three, they found them all guilty, leaving the court to sort it out. The judge's tortured logic was on full display when he declared that it "had not been proved that they were not present" and, therefore, were guilty with the rest.[94]

The *Xenia Free Press* asserted that transporting slaves across Ohio has long been in practice and was never questioned until recently. "If the right really exists," the newspaper continued, "the fact should be known and our laws amended, that our citizens may not subject themselves to fine and imprisonment for doing that which every man whose head and heart are sound must approve."[95] But if, as commonly believed, "a slave, on touching the soil of Ohio, with the consent of his master, no matter for what purpose, immediately becomes a freeman," then that should likewise be known.[96]

Nevertheless, "the trial judge advised the jury to ignore the argument that Ohio law freed the slaves automatically upon entry with the knowledge or consent of the owner. Moreover, he advised that any rescue operation was illegal under the state fugitive slave law of 1839."[97]

In all, thirteen individuals "were sentenced to the dungeon, to be fed on bread and water for five days; five of the thirteen to pay of fine of $20 each, and eight others a fine of $5 each."[98] Because the fourteenth was in poor health, he served but a few hours in the dungeon and was fined $5 as well.

Bedford wrote that the eight-foot-by-ten-foot dungeon, which already contained one prisoner, proved to be too small to accommodate them. Consequently, the constables made another room as dark as possible and placed them in it. A judge of the Supreme Court subsequently accepted a writ of error filed by the defense, and the prisoners were released forty-eight hours later to await the court's final adjudication.

In May 1841, the Supreme Court of Ohio at Lebanon reversed the lower court's judgment in the case of *State v. Farr*—(sometimes referred to as *Brooks et al v. Ohio*)—on a conviction of riot.[99] It noted that the Common Pleas Court had erred in telling the jury that acts committed after assembly could be used to conclude that they had assembled with unlawful intent.

In handing down his decision, Chief Justice Ebenezer Lane agreed with one of the rejected arguments in the Matilda case when he declared that, as long as they weren't running from their masters, slaves who set foot in Ohio were free under the law. "[I]f the owner of a slave voluntarily brings him into this state, or permit[s] him to come, although it should be only for the purpose of visiting or travelling through from one state to another, the slave in such case, becomes a free man the moment he touches the soil of Ohio."[100] Therefore, anyone attempting to deprive him of his liberty was committing an unlawful act. Fellow Justice Peter Hitchcock was in complete agreement.

Lane's purported extrajudicial remark was interpreted by Southerners as an unnecessary and unwarranted insult to slave holding states. "As it is, we are underhandedly informed that our company is not desired. Give us a bold, open enemy, to a skulking assassin any time," one Southern newspaper opined.[101] This was one of the first cases in the country to make this declaration, although it was not reported in any law reports or journals.

In 1826, Pennsylvania abolitionists pushed a law through the state legislature that established penalties for persons "who should take or carry away from the State any negro with the intention of selling him as a slave, or of detaining or causing to be detained such negro as a slave for life."[102] But this anti-kidnapping statute wasn't really put to the test until 1837, when Margarette Morgan, a fugitive slave, was arrested by Edward Prigg.

Acting on behalf of her master, Prigg transported Morgan and her children back to Maryland. He was then arrested, tried and convicted of kidnapping by authorities in Pennsylvania. His conviction was upheld on appeal by the state supreme court. But, when the case was subsequently heard by the Supreme Court of the United States in 1842, the Pennsylvania law was ruled unconstitutional.

The delay in hearing the case allowed a writ of habeas corpus to be issued, requiring Hoppess to show cause to Judge Nathaniel Reed that he had justification for holding Watson prisoner. "The case was ably opened by Mr. William Birney (a son of James G. Birney) on Wednesday…for Mr. Watson, after which court was adjourned to Saturday morning."[117]

Watson's case was then forcefully argued by William F. Johnson. That afternoon, Nathaniel C. McLean, son of Judge McLean, argued the case on behalf of Hoppess. The following Monday, another Mr. McLean, a nephew of the judge, bolstered his cousin's argument. He was followed in the afternoon by Salmon Chase, who spoke for two hours. Chase's point was "that the escape was made within the low water mark and therefore undoubtedly within the territory of Ohio."[118]

Judge Reed "then pronounced his opinion upon the various points, and in all concurred with the counsel for Mr. Hoppess."[119] He noted, in particular, that "the jurisdiction of steamers navigating the Ohio was, as far as slavery was concerned, in the State of Kentucky."[120]

Immediately, Hoppess grabbed Watson by the collar and tried to walk out of the courtroom with him. But he was stopped by Constable Rand, who refused to open the door without the magistrate's say-so. A group of volunteer constables cleared the way through the crowd in order to conduct Watson to the office of Judge Mark T. Taylor.

Brevet Major General William Birney encouraged thousands of free Black men to join the Union army. *Library of Congress.*

In the judge's office, Watson found his freedom on trial again. Once more, Birney argued on his behalf. However, when he finished, Watson realized his cause was likely lost. Turning to Birney, Watson asked, "Have you done everything—can nothing more be done?"[121] Birney replied that he had. "God Almighty bless you, then, Mr. Birney!" Watson said, "I'll never forget you!"[122] Within a few minutes, Judge Taylor allowed Hoppess to take Watson to Kentucky. Despite losing the case, Salmon Chase was presented with a silver pitcher "by the colored people of Cincinnati" on May 6, 1845, in appreciation for his efforts on their behalf."[123]

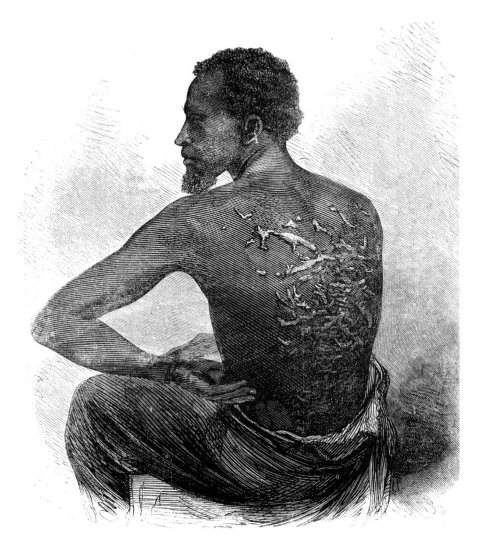

The cruelty of some Southern slaveholders shocked many people in the North. *Authors' collection.*

Four years later, when the abolitionists gained the upper hand in Hamilton County, Judge Reed, an "erratic genius" according to his contemporaries, lost his seat on the bench. He passed away in 1853 at the age of forty-three, succumbing to what his contemporaries deemed "that vice which has proved a destroyer of so many men."[124] Alcohol, presumably.

# 5

# GAY LUCK TO OUR HUNTERS

*Gay luck to our hunters! how nobly they ride*
*In the glow of their zeal, and the strength of their pride!*
—*John Greenleaf Whittier, "The Hunters of Men"*

On the night of October 25, 1844, six people who were being held in slavery fled the plantation of Peter Driskell in Maysville, Kentucky. As soon as he realized they were missing, Driskell executed a power of attorney and delivered it to Charles S. Mitchell, authorizing him to act as his agent to recapture the fugitives. Mitchell's fee was $1.25 a day and expenses.

Accompanied by Andrew Jackson Driskell—Peter's son—and Alexander B. Martin, Colonel Mitchell started north in pursuit of the runaways. They were seeking Jane Garrison, about forty years old; Bob, about seventeen; Mary, nearly sixteen; Dock (aka "Docktor" or "Ben"), nearly eighteen; Will (aka "Williams" or "Bill"), between eleven and twelve; and Harrison, between four and five. But rain had obliterated all traces of the escapees' trail. It would take Mitchell and his party three months to track them down.

At noon on February 28, 1845, Will and Dock were apprehended in Sandusky, Ohio—some 230 miles north. They were charged with being fugitives from service. Two days earlier, Mitchell spotted Will near the tavern, where he and the others was staying. In order to discover the whereabouts of the others, he paid a small boy to play marbles with Will and pump him for information.

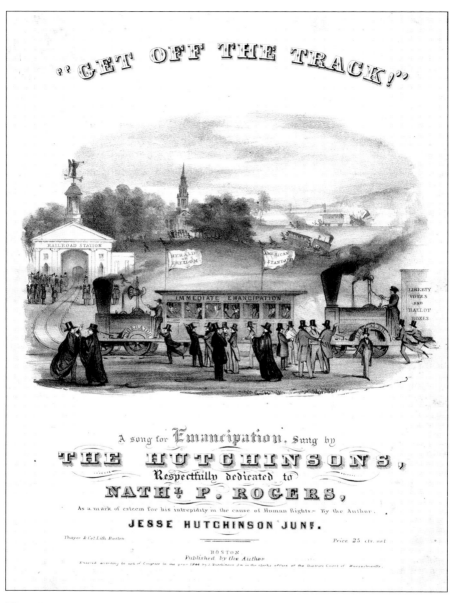

The railroad to emancipation had become a metaphor by 1844 as this song illustrates. *Library of Congress.*

The Kentuckians subsequently snatched one of the young men off the street while he was fetching water and grabbed the other from a wood house where he was sawing wood. They then took them to an upper room in the Mansion House hotel where they were kept under watch. Will admitted that Jane and her son, Harrison, were residing in the Frank D. Parish household. Not long after they arrived in Sandusky, the two had presented themselves to Parish and he promptly hired Jane as a servant.

Early that afternoon, Mitchell set off for the Parish residence and happened to encounter Frank Parish along the way. He asked Parish if Jane and Harrison were at his home, and he replied that they were. Mitchell then asked if he could see them, and Parish said he could if Jane wished it. When they arrived at the house, Mitchell said he wanted to speak with both mother and son, but Parish wouldn't allow either of them to approach him. Mitchell then informed Parish that they were slaves of Peter Driskell, and he wanted to return them to Kentucky.

"By what authority?" Parish asked.

"By the power of attorney from Peter Driskell," Mitchell replied, reaching for the document in his breast pocket. But Parish said he would require judicial authority before he would allow them to be arrested. Parish then "shoved [the mother and son] into the house, went in himself, and closed the door after him."[125]

The abduction of Will and Dock did not go unnoticed. Mitchell, Driskell and Martin were soon arrested on a writ of habeas corpus issued by Justice Z.W. Barker. Upon examination by Barker with the assistance of Mayor E.B. Sadler, the three men were ordered to post appearance bonds of one hundred dollars each on a charge of riot.

After Parish swore out an affidavit alleging that Will and Dock had been unlawfully detained, Associate Judge Moors Farwell issued writs of habeas corpus for them as well. Proceeding to the Mansion House, the sheriff took custody of the two teenagers and lodged them in jail to await the outcome of the proceedings.

At a hearing before Farwell on Monday, Parish and Lucas S. Beecher served as counsel for the two young men, while John Wheeler and John N. Sloane represented the claimants.[126] Parish and Beecher sought, among other things, to question "whether the constitution intended to authorize the owner to [delegate] his authority to another, and pursue his remedy by an agent."[127] However, the *Sandusky Clarion* cited language in the Ordinance of 1787—"which all acknowledge to be equal if not superior validity to the constitution"—as support of the slaveholder's right to do so.

On cross-examination, the kidnappers admitted that they had "no knowledge of the actual purchase of the woman and child, except by hearsay; [did] not know but that Driskell paid them wages, nor but that they had permission to leave."[128] After weighing the evidence, Farwell said, "That Ohio being a free state, all our presumptions are in favor of liberty; and that to authorize a removal under the constitution and laws, every point must be provided step by step, according to the principles of common law."[129] In the judge's opinion, Mitchell and Driskell failed to show just cause for the capture and detention of the youths, so he set them free. He also ordered the men to pay court costs.

No sooner had the decision been handed down than Dock and Will were sprung from jail and transported to Canada, where Jane and Harrison were waiting. Credit was roundly given to Parish for his quick action in disrupting the plans of the slave hunters. However, he had little time to savor his victory before Driskell brought suit against him for the monetary value of the mother and son.[130] Furthermore, not everyone was pleased with what had transpired.

On March 6, 1845, the Erie County Courthouse was host to a large meeting of some of Sandusky's "best citizens."[131] The meeting's purpose was "to correct an erroneous impression that the citizens of Sandusky are so generally abolitionists that they offer every facility to the fugitive to make good his escape."[132]

When *Driskell v. Parish* was heard by the U.S. Circuit Court of Ohio during the November 1847 term, Colonel Mitchell was the key witness. He testified that he was an acquaintance of Peter Driskell. They lived about three-quarters of a mile apart, six miles outside Maysville, Kentucky. He said that Jane and Harrison were Mitchell's slaves, along with four other children born to her. When he informed Parish of that fact, he expected him to surrender the fugitives as required by law.

Sandusky Bay became the passage to Canada for many fugitives from bondage. *Authors' collection.*

However, a Miss Dastin, who witnessed the exchange between Mitchell and Parish, testified that "there was no demand for arrest, no pushing of the servants into the house, no attempt by Mitchell to seize, and prevention of seizure by Parish."[133]

"Upon the trial, Mr. [Salmon] Chase, with Mr. I.W. Andrews of Columbus, defended Mr. Parish. There was no evidence in the case against him, except that of Mitchell and Driskell; and the whole of it related to the transaction at Mr. Parish's house."[134] Nevertheless, a jury found him guilty of obstructing justice and ordered him to pay the sum of $500, the proven value of the slaves. Including costs and expenses, the judgment against Parish totaled $1,000, which was paid by his abolitionist friends.

Despite being the capital of a free state, Columbus was home to many Southern sympathizers. Take William Henderson for example. He was seated in his law office on Friday, March 27, 1846, when Alexander Forbes entered and presented him with a power of attorney authorizing Forbes "to arrest a certain fugitive from labor, a negro man by the name of Jerry, or Jerry Finney."[135] The document had been witnessed by two men and certified by Henry Wingate, the presiding judge of Franklin County, Kentucky.[136]

Henderson was not his first choice. Forbes had first applied to Judge Joseph R. Swan of Columbus but was turned away. An abolitionist, Judge Swan would go on to help found the Republican Party a few years later.[137] The slave hunter then made his way to Henderson's office, just across the Scioto River in Franklinton. In his capacity as an acting justice of the peace for Franklin Township, Henderson proved to be more agreeable. He would later remark that "the magistrates in Columbus were 'a set of damned abolitionists' who would not give Forbes justice."[138]

Satisfied that the documents were in order, Henderson began preparing the necessary paperwork, while Forbes left to meet with his confederates to set his plan in motion. Between seven and eight o'clock that evening, Jerry arrived at Henderson's office, accompanied by a Black youth. He had been instructed by a couple of men to deliver a trunk to Henderson's office from a Columbus hotel. They claimed that a young couple were going to be secretly wed there and would be leaving on their honeymoon immediately afterward. One of the men was Jacob Armitage, whom Finney knew and trusted.

When Jerry admitted himself into the office, he found it was dark except for the dim glow of the stove. But a handful of men were waiting for him inside. In addition to Armitage and Henderson, there were Henry Henderson (William's brother), David A. Potter, Daniel Zinn and John Stephenson (or Stevenson). They were immediately joined by Forbes, who locked the door, grabbed Finney and clamped a hand over his mouth, stifling his screams. Potter and Stephenson then bound and secured Finney with handcuffs, before placing him under arrest as a fugitive slave.

Finney asked for a fair trial. He told them he had witnesses who could attest to the fact that he was a free man. But Justice Henderson replied that the document Forbes had in his possession was all that was necessary. Forbes then swore an oath that the man they had taken into custody was the person he had been seeking and signed an affidavit attesting to the same. Henderson produced a certificate authorizing Forbes to convey Jerry back to his owner in Kentucky. In exchange, Forbes handed Henderson a payment of ten dollars—less than the magistrate expected, but he was assured he would receive the balance soon enough. The whole affair lasted less than thirty minutes.

Jerry purportedly admitted that he was formerly enslaved in Kentucky but had been brought to Ohio either by his owner or with his owner's consent. Therefore, he was, he insisted, entitled to his freedom. Nevertheless, he was quickly spirited off in Zinn's awaiting carriage. Taken to London, some twenty-five miles southwest of Columbus, Jerry was then transferred to a stagecoach. The other passengers on the stage, some of whom knew him, were of "the opinion that he was drugged, as all attempts to draw him into conversation or to get the facts from him unavailing, and he even failed to recognize some who had long known him."[139] The slave catchers told them he was a horse-thief and had passed counterfeit money.

The youth who had accompanied Jerry to Henderson's office had been detained another two to three hours to give the kidnappers time to escape with their prisoner. As soon as he was released, he raised the alarm. Saturday morning, the city of Columbus was in an uproar over the kidnapping of Jerry Finney. As the *Ohio State Journal* reported, "Our city was thrown into the greatest excitement this morning, by intelligence that a respectable and peaceable colored man, who has been residing here between twelve and sixteen years, was enticed across the bridge to the town of Franklinton, last evening, and there handcuffed, gagged and forcibly placed into a vehicle to be taken to Kentucky."[140]

According to several historians, Jerry was well known "at nearly all the hotels and houses of entertainment [in the city], having been cook and general waiter or servant."[141] Governor Mordecai Bartley immediately issued a warrant for the arrest of Forbes and Armitage, and a number of men set out in pursuit of them. Riding swift horses, they followed the slave hunters to Xenia, where they learned they had boarded a train for Cincinnati. Still

Free Black people were sometimes abducted by bands of slave hunters who were enabled by corrupt officials. *Library of Congress.*

hoping to overtake them, they raced on. However, they arrived just minutes after the kidnappers had been transported safely across the Ohio River by mail boat and were on their way to Frankfort.

Arrest warrants were soon issued for Squire Henderson, Henry Henderson, Jacob Armitage, Daniel A. Potter and Daniel Zinn on charges of aiding and abetting the alleged kidnapping. All but Armitage and Zinn were promptly apprehended and brought before Columbus mayor Alexander Patton for a hearing. The courthouse was packed until late in the evening when the trio were carted off to prison. Failing to post the $500 bail, the prisoners would remain there until they went to trial at the next term of the court of common pleas. A fourth man, Stephenson, made an affidavit against the trio but then fled the area to avoid possible prosecution for his involvement in the affair.

On the evening of March 31, a meeting was held—one of the largest ever in Columbus. Citizens packed the Town Street Methodist Episcopal Church to hear several spirited addresses delivered by Samuel Galloway, Reverend Granville Moody, and others. There was a profound sense of outrage which animated the crowd. Resolutions were adopted fiercely denouncing Finney's abduction and all connected with it, and expressing a determination "to rescue him from the scoundrels who stole him from his family."[142]

Because Forbes and Armitage had left the state, Governor Bartley issued a requisition for their arrest to the governor of Kentucky on the evening of April 1, 1846. He also planned to issue a proclamation announcing a reward for the kidnappers but was awaiting the results of the proceedings. The citizens of Columbus raised $500 to add to the $500 already proposed by the governor.

In response to Bartley's warrant, Kentucky governor William Owsley commanded the sheriff to arrest Forbes and Armitage. On April 10, 1846, the two men were taken before Judge Mason Brown, a circuit court justice, to ascertain whether they had been operating within the provisions of Kentucky law. The two questions to be answered were: (1) Was Jerry Finney a slave? And (2) if so, were Forbes and Armitage authorized to act on behalf of his owner?

Attorney William Johnston of Cincinnati was dispatched by Governor Bartley to represent Ohio's interests. While serving in the Ohio House of Representatives, Johnston was given the nickname "Booby" by newspaper publisher Samuel Medary—a staunch peace Democrat—and it was adopted by his friends. However, Johnston was no "booby" when it came to law, where he had a reputation for his eloquent and persuasive presentations in the courtroom.

During the hearing, evidence was introduced which substantiated that Finney was the property of Mrs. Bathsheba (or Bethsheba) D. Long of Frankfort, Kentucky. How she came to own another human being was a complicated story that began many years earlier with Hezekiah Brown. Born in Virginia, Brown had served as a private in the Continental army. Following the death of his first wife, Anne Stubblefield, he married Sarah Long, widow of Brumfield Long. Included among the property she brought with her to the marriage was Rose, an enslaved woman whom she had inherited from her late husband.

In 1799, Brown bought one thousand acres on the Kentucky River near Frankfort, the capital city of the commonwealth. Later, Rose gave birth to a son who would take the name Jeremiah "Jerry" Finney (or Phinney). Upon his death in 1821, Brown's will stipulated that he was *loaning* Sarah, his widow, "the boy Jerry, to be held during her natural life, and after her death to go to her heirs."[143]

A month later, Sarah deeded all shares and interest in the estate of her first husband, Brumfield Long, to her son, Thomas. Not more than three

There is no way to know how many runaways failed in their attempt to reach freedom. *Authors' collection.*

years afterward, Sarah is believed to have passed away as well, and the rights to Jerry fell to her children. Each of them, apparently, received some portion of twenty-seven shares in the young man. One of nine children, Thomas proceeded to purchase the interests of all but three of his siblings in his mother's estate and left everything to his third wife, Bathsheba D. Moxley, upon his death in 1826. Bathsheba would live for another forty-four years.[144]

Over the next few years, Bathsheba purchased the remaining interests in Jerry, save for one-third of a share. She was now 26/27ths owner of another human being. However, about 1830–31, she had allowed a gambler named Allgaier to hire Jerry to work on a farm in Woodford County. He purportedly promised never to remove the slave from Kentucky, but then took him to Cincinnati for a period of six months. When Bathsheba learned of it, she wrote Allgaier a letter demanding that he return him at once or risk being sued. Allgaier did as she directed.

Several weeks later, Jerry asked his owner if he could return to Ohio in order to fetch some articles of clothing he had left behind. Bathsheba gave him a pass to do so, and he never came back. She subsequently advertised him as a runaway slave, offering a reward for his apprehension. On three separate occasions, she had executed a power of attorney to three different slave catchers, but without success.

After making good his escape, Finney purportedly taunted Bathsheba and his other owners by sending them papers with insulting messages written in the margins. One such inscription read,

> *Please send me a statement of my exact age, and by doing so, you will confer a very particular favor on your very particular friend,*

*JEREMIAH PHINNEY.*

> *P.S. I've improved in writing very fast, since I left Frankfort, haven't I?*[145]

Charles S. Morehead, attorney for Forbes and Armitage and a man of deeply held prejudices, subsequently maintained that since Jerry was a slave and the two men had the proper authority to arrest him, they could not be guilty of any crime for doing so.[146]

Johnston, on the other hand, asserted that "the Kentucky statute was contrary to the Constitution of the United States, and that slavery, being contrary to natural law, existed only by municipal law, and being thus local and confined to the territorial limits within which it is sanctioned, a slave once free is always free."[147] He also sought to establish that, since Jerry had been hired by Allgaier and taken to Ohio, he had not escaped from his owner. Rather, he had been freed by the simple act of having been brought to Ohio. What's more, Forbes and Armitage had taken him in violation of the law and were, therefore, guilty of kidnapping and should be returned to Ohio for trial.

Although Johnston argued the case masterfully, after two days the court found against him, ending all legal proceedings. Judge Mason Brown ruled that the constitutionality of Kentucky law was not a matter for his court to consider. Having established that Jerry was the property of Bathsheba Long, he asserted that both Forbes and Armitage were protected by the laws of the state when they apprehended him on her behalf.[148]

Meanwhile, the Henderson brothers and Potter were worried about their situation in Ohio. In their own defense, they wrote several letters that were circulated in Kentucky and published in various newspapers, appealing to the citizens of Kentucky to protect them. Henderson described how Forbes came to his office and presented him with a power of attorney, making him "an authorized agent to arrest a certain fugitive from labor, a negro man by the name of Jerry, or Jerry Finney."[149]

However, Henderson realized that, if the power of attorney was not in order, "it will go very hard with us and is a perjury on the said Forbes."[150] He begged Mrs. Long to provide him with proof of her ownership of Finney because, "The Abolitionists of this place are determined that we shall be convicted of kidnapping."[151]

As expected, in July 1846, a grand jury in Franklin County indicted Forbes for abduction of Jerry and indicted Armitage, Henderson and the others as aiders and abettors in the kidnapping. Later in the month, Constable Brown, Mr. Cherry and a gentleman from Franklinton brought Jacob Armitage to Columbus and turned him over to the sheriff. They had found him the previous night at the home of a Mr. Fleming in Prairie Township. He was thought to have been on the way to Columbus to give himself up because he did not want the warrant for his arrest hanging over his head. Armitage posted $750 in bail and was released.

William Henderson and the others—except for Forbes, who had not been arrested—were tried at a special session of the Franklin County Court of Common Pleas in September. A.F. Perry and future Ohio governor William Dennison Jr. conducted the prosecution, while F. J. Matthews and Colonel Noah H. Swayne, a devout Quaker, handled the defense.[152]

"The trial excited much interest in the city and abroad," a local historian recalled.[153] Two days were given over to impaneling the jury. It took more than a week to hear all of the testimony. Arguments of the counsel and the charge to the jury took another couple of days. The case hinged on whether Squire Henderson, in his capacity as a justice of the peace, had acted in good faith. While the trial was in progress, Dr. George Richey, one of the jurors, fell sick and could no longer attend. So, it was agreed by everyone involved to proceed with the eleven remaining jurors.

"After deliberating seven hours the jury returned a verdict finding Justice Henderson guilty, and acquitting all the other defendants on the ground…that those acquitted were ignorant of the law and of the facts as to Finney's freedom."[154] Henderson was remanded to jail, while the others went free. However, the court suspended sentencing while Henderson's attorneys took the case up with the Ohio Supreme Court on writ of error.

A devout Quaker, Noah H. Swayne replaced his friend John McLean on the U.S. Supreme Court. *Library of Congress.*

At the January 1847 session, Chief Justice Wood pronounced what was understood to be a unanimous opinion of the court. Among the errors were, first, the withdrawal of a juror (Richey) in a criminal case by consent while the trial proceeded. Second, "That Henderson, being a Justice of the Peace, acted in a judicial capacity, and had jurisdiction in the case of an escaping slave, and consequently, his proceedings could not be called in question, for not acting in good faith, as he would be protected by the doctrine of judicial immunity."[155] And third, because of his judicial immunity, he would not be liable to indictment, but could be called in question only by impeachment.

Throughout the summer, Jerry Finney remained in Kentucky, confined in the Kentucky State Penitentiary at Frankfort. Although they had been unsuccessful in liberating him through the court system, his friends back in Columbus did not give up. Taking up a collection, they purchased his freedom from his owner for $550, despite concerns by other slaveholders in Frankfort that it would encourage other slaves to escape. But it was agreed that the money would be refunded if it could be proved that he was legally a free man.

On September 18, 1846, nearly six months after his abduction, Jerry found himself on his way home to Columbus—a free man once again. But he was in poor health, having contracted consumption while imprisoned. As a result, he died not long after being reunited with his family.

Although Jerry's kidnapping was planned by Kentuckians, they had only been able to carry it out with the assistance of certain Ohioans. As the *Anti-Slavery Bugle* opined, "Let the guilt be placed where it belongs; let the people of Ohio be made to feel that if men can be stolen from their soil with impunity, it is because they will it to be so."[156]

# 6

# THE SAINT AND THE SINNER

*The saint and the sinner, with cursing and prayer,*
*The drunk and the sober, ride merrily there.*
—*John Greenleaf Whittier, "The Hunters of Men"*

Reflecting the shift in public sentiment, the Ohio legislature finally repealed the state's Black Laws on February 10, 1849. Specifically, the act of 1807, which had been reenacted four different times. However, the mood in Washington, D.C., was different. Ever since the passage of the original Fugitive Slave Act of 1793, the pro-slavery faction had been agitating to strengthen it. On September 18, 1850, Congress passed the Compromise of 1850 in exchange for California's admission to the Union as a free state.

Of the five separate bills, one was a harsher Fugitive Slave Act. Designed to placate the South, this new law effectively put the rights of slaveholders above those of other American citizens by compelling them to assist in the capture of runaway slaves or risk criminal punishment. It also denied those accused of being fugitives the right to a jury trial or even the right to testify in his or her own defense.

President Zachary Taylor had opposed the package of bills, but "Old Rough and Ready," as he was dubbed for his military exploits, died suddenly and somewhat mysteriously. His successor, President Millard Fillmore, disliked slavery, but he felt that the federal government could not do away with it. His primary concern was with preserving the Union, so he signed the compromise without hesitation.

President Zachary Taylor tried to rise above politics by not picking a side on any issue.
*Library of Congress.*

Although opposed to slavery, President Millard Fillmore signed the Fugitive Slave Law to preserve the Union. *Library of Congress.*

Arguably, the new fugitive slave law had exactly the opposite effect of what its supporters had hoped—it increased the number of runaways. It also may have made abolitionists out of thousands of Americans who previously were indifferent to slavery. One Columbus, Ohio newspaper declared that the federal government had now dedicated itself to "Life, Liberty, and the Pursuit of Niggers."[157] But for the Polly family, things could hardly have gotten any worse. They were already in a fight for their lives.

Peyton Polly (some sources say Polley or Pauley) was the patriarch of the Polly clan and a former slave. He was once enslaved by David Polly of Pike County, Kentucky. According to historian James Hale, when David drew up his will in 1837, he provided for his slaves to be freed upon his death. But after his wife passed away, he revised it, leaving his entire estate to his Black bondservants: Peyton, Douglas ("Duglas" or "Dug"), John, Spencer, Jude, Mirah and William. There are intimations he may have been the father of one or more of them.

Predictably, when David died in 1847, the will was contested by those shirttail relations who felt they were his rightful heirs. A settlement was reached in which the slaves gained their freedom but lost any claim on their inheritance. With no resources of their own, the formerly enslaved members of the Polly family found work locally.

By January 20, 1849, Douglas and Peyton had saved enough money to purchase Peyton's wife, Violet, and at least seven children held by David and Nancy Polly Campbell. A receipt for $800 was made out to Douglas. As stipulated in the terms of sale, Douglas took the Polly slaves to Ohio and freed them. They settled in Rock Camp, Lawrence County, just above Burlington. Many Black men had obtained work there in the local iron furnaces.[158]

Because David Campbell was a bad businessman and possibly an alcoholic, his creditors grew concerned that he would not be able to pay them. When they began to pressure him, Campbell denied having received any cash from Douglas and Peyton, only promissory notes.

"The creditors became outraged and declared the sale of the slaves a scam sale," Hale wrote, "a fraudulent maneuver to maintain possession of the slaves."[159] They sued both the Campbells and the Pollys for what they were owed. Douglas was forced to pay Campbell's creditors $550 (or possibly $1,500), including fines. Additionally, the ownership of the oldest son, Nathan, was handed over to George Brown of Pike County in lieu of $125. But it didn't end there. Campbell's brother-in-law, David Justice—"a kidnapping, swindling slave dealer," to quote Hale—created a phony bill of sale.[160]

Fortunately, the court in Ohio rejected his bogus claim that the Pollys were fugitive slaves. But David Justice wasn't about to let the law get in his way. He hired "three or four desperate fellows"—Fildon Isaac, James Sperry, Washington Smith and Hamilton Willis—to kidnap them for him.[161]

As historian Jonathan Wells related, "On March 6, 1850, the day before Massachusetts senator Daniel Webster would deliver his famous speech in favor of the Fugitive Slave Act, a gang of white kidnappers axed their way into Polly's home, beat him severely, and dragged his eight young charges across the border into Kentucky."[162] (Sources differ. It may have actually been June 6, 1850.)[163] The men took Hulda, Douglas, Peyton Jr., Harrison, Nelson, Louisa, Anna and a granddaughter, Mary Jane, while leaving behind Peyton Polly and his wife, Violet, likely because they were elderly.

A Lawrence County abolitionist quickly called for Ohio governor Seabury Ford to intervene. Because Peyton was "a pauper of color" who couldn't afford to initiate legal proceedings to recover his children, the state took action on his behalf. Having campaigned against slavery, Ford issued a requisition to the governor of Kentucky, demanding the release of the Polly children and the return of the kidnappers to Ohio for prosecution. But Ford's term was ending. His successor, Reuben Wood, was a Democrat who made it clear that he was acting more out of a sense of duty than belief in the cause. By that time, the children had been split up, with four going to Frankfort, Kentucky, and the other four to a slave owner in Virginia.

On March 4, 1851, Governor Wood appointed General Joel W. Wilson of Seneca County to handle the matter. Wilson, in turn, hired three Kentucky attorneys. The *Cincinnati Enquirer* observed, "If the case comes to trial it will involve some points of law that it will be well to have immediately decided."[164] Meanwhile, Ralph Leete, a Lawrence County attorney, had taken it upon himself to become involved in the case. But as historian Stephen Middleton observed, "Those officials moved slowly, and more than three years elapsed before Leete received any reliable information about the Polly children."[165]

When Leete discovered that Justice had kept the children—Hulda, Peyton Jr., Mary Jane and a fourth named Martha—near Maynard, Kentucky, locked in his own jail, he filed paperwork in the relevant court, demanding their release. But still the foot-dragging continued.

"After protracted litigation in various courts of that State, four of the negroes were declared free by the Court of Appeal in 1853, and returned to their friends in Ohio."[166] (This does not square with an earlier report that Governor Wood had learned that one of the Polly family members had been returned to Ohio in November 1851.) Nevertheless, the governor, "who took a deep interest in reclaiming these kidnapped negroes, speaks highly of the Kentuckians in this trial," the newspapers claimed.[167]

To represent Ohio's interests in the Virginia courts, Wilson hired John Saidley of Guyandotte, Virginia. But Attorney Leroy D. Walton was subsequently assigned to pursue the case. Walton then hired J. Frey, who was able to determine that the Polly children were in the custody of slave owner William "Squire" Ratcliffe in Wayne County.

Ratcliffe had a bill of sale, albeit a phony one, for the children. But the men from whom he purchased them were hiding out in the hills and threatened harm to anyone who came after them. One of the biggest obstacles to rescuing the Polly children was that Virginia officials did not believe that Ohio had the right to automatically free slaves who entered the state. Therefore, they supported Ratcliffe's claim on the four Polly children, even if it was fraudulent.

The more the Polly family heard about the conditions under which the children were being held, the more they despaired. Not only were the young ones being mistreated, but also the eldest daughter had been raped and was pregnant. Furthermore, another of the four kidnap victims had passed away while being held in captivity. However, the birth of the rape victim's child kept their number at four.

According to a memorandum in the files of Ohio governor Salmon Chase, "In 1853 they were declared free by the Court of Cabell county Virginia; but the defendants appealed on the ground of Jurisdiction, and the higher court decided that the cases should have been tried in Wayne instead of Cabell county—Wayne being the actual residence of the defendant in the case."[168]

As a result, a weary John Saidley asked that "Ralph Seete" (Leete) be officially appointed to assist him. Learning the direction the buyer was taking them, he secured the services of yet another lawyer and headed for Louisville. His plan was to arrest everyone involved and submit the case to trial.

In a letter to Governor Chase dated July 25, 1856, Leete provided a summary of the case so far. He was clearly frustrated by the legal maneuverings in Virginia but insisted, "It is wrong to let the case be abandoned now; if the Federal Government could spend $100,000 to reduce one man to slavery, certainly the State of Ohio should not withhold the necessary amount of means to restore three persons [allowing for the one death] to freedom."[169]

Nine years after the Pollys were abducted, a Virginia court dismissed the case entirely, declaring that only the Polly children and not the State of Ohio could sue Ratcliffe. It was now 1859, and as one Virginia resident observed, "the colored children are very much attached to Ratcliffe and his family."[170]

Leete wrote in a letter dated November 25, 1859:

*The case in Virginia has been bungled and shamefully mismanaged from the commencement. I had the management of the cases in KY, which were taken to the Court of Appeals in that State and in 1853 got a decree, that sent four of the kidnapped children home to this county where they now reside. [M]y opinion is that some additional counsel should be employed in the Va. case.*[171]

By the time Republican governor William Dennison took over in January 1860, Leete was ready to give up. And, with the outbreak of the Civil War in 1861, the case became moot. The four kidnapped members

Governor William Dennison Jr. refused to return fugitive slaves to Kentucky and Virginia. *Library of Congress.*

of the Polly family—some no longer children—would remain enslaved until the hostilities came to an end and the Confederacy dissolved.

Dr. Christopher Graham firmly believed that he provided his slaves with a good life. In 1819, he had gone to Harrodsburg, Kentucky, to start his medical practice. Within the first year, he married the daughter of David Sutton, a local landowner, and opened Harrodsburg Springs, a health resort. Very soon thereafter, he acquired another spring and renamed the complex Graham Springs. Among the improvements he made over the next several decades were the addition of a bandstand, a ballroom, several bathhouses, a bowling alley, a badminton court, two rows of cabins and a four-story hotel.

Graham Springs became a popular destination for those seeking the supposed healthful benefits of its mineral springs. Under Graham's guidance, it also became known for its fancy dress and masquerade balls. Graham took particular pride in his band of enslaved musicians: Henry, George and Reuben. They entertained the guests at Graham Springs during the summer months and were hired out to perform elsewhere during the winter.

Henry was a self-taught fiddling prodigy. Graham had purchased him from his father-in-law, David Sutton, for $750, several times the going rate for a fourteen-year-old boy. He then paired him up with two other slaves he owned: George, who played fiddle and guitar, and Reuben, who had taught himself the banjo. In addition to working as dining room servants, these "three yellow men," as Graham described them, played at various entertainments in a band led by Henry Williams, a free Black man who lived in Louisville.[172]

When a recession caused Dr. Graham to shutter his spa early in 1837, he agreed to allow Henry and Reuben to join Williams and his band in Louisville. This was formalized in a document dated August 30, 1837:

*This is to give liberty to my boys, Henry and Reuben, to go to Louisville, with Williams and to play with him till I may wish to call them home. Should Williams find it in his interest to take them to Cincinnati, New Albany, or any part of the South, even so far as New Orleans, he is at liberty to do so.*[173]

Graham referred to them as "slaves for life," as well as "faithful and hard-working servants."[174] He did not believe he had any reason to question their loyalty because he had always been good to them.

Once Henry and Reuben joined him, Williams concentrated on improving their musicianship. When he was satisfied with the results, they began playing jobs in Louisville, then branched out to New Albany and Madison Indiana, and Cincinnati, Ohio. This necessitated traveling by ferry or steamboat and sometimes staying away from home for several nights. As a result, they became well known to the operators of the river vessels.

In 1839, Dr. Graham notified Williams that he wanted Henry and Reuben to return to Harrodsburg, where they were reunited with George. Instead of keeping them there, Graham set them up in Lexington. He empowered the trio to book their own engagements, collect the payments and, after paying their own expenses, turn the profits over to him. However, Graham suspected this taste of freedom was eroding their loyalty to him. While he vacationed in New Orleans during the winter of 1840–41, the musicians began planning their escape. It was during this period that they met another enslaved man with plans of his own.

Milton Clarke was visiting Louisville, Kentucky, when he learned that his sister had died, leaving him her property. It was enough that he could use it to purchase his freedom as well as that of his siblings. But he was warned that if he took any action to acquire the property, his owner could claim it as his own. Instead, Clarke asked his master, Deacon A. Logan in Lexington, Kentucky, to set him free. He offered to pay him $1,000—money he expected to receive from his late sister's estate. Logan refused. But he gave Clarke the necessary paperwork so that he could travel freely up and down the Ohio River to conduct whatever business he chose.

After going to New Orleans and then to Galveston, Clarke returned to Louisville. It was there he met "Henry, Reuben, and George; all smart, fine fellows, good musicians, and yielding [Dr. Graham] a handsome income."[175] After telling them he intended to go to Ohio the next day to seek his freedom, Clarke invited them to join him. They then bought passage on the steamer *Pike*, under the pretense of having been hired to play at a grand ball in Cincinnati. Upon reaching Cincinnati, Graham's slaves continued on to Canada while Clarke went to Oberlin, where he met up with his brother Lewis.

When Dr. Graham failed to receive his monthly payment from the trio, he looked into it and discovered they had not been seen since they took a stagecoach to Louisville. He then contacted Williams, but the bandleader said he had not seen anything of the three men since they played a job there. Consequently, Graham placed ads in a number of newspapers, offering a reward for the return of the three.

When he reached Detroit, Graham discovered that his slaves had crossed the ice to Malden, Canada, on the Detroit River.[176] Clarke later wrote that Graham failed in several attempts to hire someone to go to Malden and abduct them. Finally, he found one person who agreed to call on them in an attempt to lure them onto a boat to Toledo. The plan was for Graham to arrest them as soon as they were on board.

"When the wolf in sheep's clothing offered them five hundred dollars to go and play for one ball," Clarke recalled, "they were more suspicious than ever."[177] Instead, as the boat docked in Malden, the three men played a gypsy waltz, a tune that was one of Graham's favorites. The doctor spent the next several days trying to persuade them to return to Kentucky with him. He simply could not understand why they would prefer to live as free men.

Under Kentucky law, Dr. Graham could hold the owners of the steamer *Pike* liable for the loss of his three slaves, so he filed a bill against Jacob Strader and John Gorman (both of Ohio), owners of the boat, and John Armstrong, its captain, in the Louisville Chancery Court in October 1844. He charged them with unauthorized transport of his slaves, whom he valued at $1,500 each. The court, however, dismissed the complaint with respect to Henry and Reuben, ruling that the written agreement previously signed with Williams was sufficient to cover their passage on the steamboat. However, there was no agreement regarding George, so the jury awarded Dr. Graham $1,000 (or perhaps $3,000) in damages.

In the Kentucky Court of Appeals, the defense argued that the three slaves had often traveled on the *Pike* as though they were free, so Armstrong naturally assumed they were. Strader and Gorman had no personal knowledge of the incident because they were not on board at the time. It was further argued that the slaves had gained their freedom by traveling to Indiana and Ohio as stipulated in the Northwest Ordinance of 1787. However, the court ruled for Graham, holding that the slaves' brief sojourns to Ohio and Indiana had not changed their status in Kentucky.

In 1851, ten years after Harry, Reuben and George escaped from slavery, the case of *Strader v. Graham* reached the United States Supreme Court. "The steamboat owners, Strader and Gorman, appealed the case…on a writ of error."[178] The justices thoroughly debated the constitutional questions before reversing the lower court's decision regarding Henry and Reuben and remanding the case back to Kentucky for retrial.

In an opinion by Chief Justice Taney, the court held that it lacked jurisdiction to review the Kentucky court's ruling because this ruling was based entirely on state law.

> *There is nothing in the Constitution of the United States that can in any degree control the law of Kentucky upon this subject. And the condition of the negroes, therefore, as to freedom or slavery, after their returned, depended altogether upon the laws of that State, and could not be influenced by the laws of Ohio.*[179]

**PRACTICAL ILLUSTRATION OF THE FUGITIVE SLAVE LAW.**

The Fugitive Slave Law served to further divide a country that had not yet found its footing. *Library of Congress.*

Both rulings—on the jurisdictional point and on the slaves' status—were later relied on by the justices in their opinions in *Dred Scott*.

The first fugitive slave case tried in Cincinnati under the new Fugitive Slave Law was on February 10, 1851, and it caused great excitement. Since the slave, Fanny, was brought to Ohio by her master, her attorneys maintained that she was entitled to her freedom. She had been arrested on the wharf and placed in the watch house for safekeeping. As the *Cincinnati Gazette* reported, "While there awaiting the issue of a warrant by Mr. Carpenter, United States Commissioner, a writ of habeas corpus was granted by Judge [R.B.] Warden, of the Common Pleas Court."[180]

Taken before Commissioner Samuel S. Carpenter the following morning, both sides were provided with the opportunity to state their cases. Testimony established that Fanny, age twenty-one or so, and a servant boy, nineteen, came down the Ohio River with their owner, William Hutchinson, on the steamer *Cumberland Valley* (or perhaps *Cumberland Belle*). Having traveled from their home in Clarksville, Tennessee (alternately, Todd County, Kentucky), they had boarded the boat in Salines, [West] Virginia. They docked at about four o'clock on Monday morning.

Later that day, Fanny accompanied Hutchinson into the city to do some shopping. As they were returning to the steamer, a stranger engaged Hutchinson in conversation. At some point, Fanny disappeared. When Hutchinson realized she was missing, he and "his friend, Mr. Boyd," set out to find her. Although they overtook her, "the interference of bystanders prevented a summary reclamation, and the attempt resulted in a row in which blowers were passed freely."[181] She was later discovered hiding in a stateroom of the steamer *Lancaster*, which was scheduled to depart ahead of the *Cumberland Valley*.[182]

While they were still on the boat, it started upriver. Although Hutchinson and Boyd asked that they all be put ashore on the Ohio side, the captain of the *Lancaster* refused to do, feeling that it might cause trouble. Instead, he landed near Newport, Kentucky. From there, the two men and the young woman took a ferry back to Cincinnati. As they walked back to the *Cumberland Valley*, which was moored at the foot of Main Street, they found themselves surrounded by a mob. When the opportunity presented itself, several abolitionists grabbed the girl and rushed her to a nearby watch house.

One or two officers who had custody of Fanny testified that she had told them that she wanted to be returned to her master. When Judge Warden asked if she wanted to go with her master or be free, "She replied that she wished to be free."[183] Attorneys Donn Piatt, Stanley Mathews and Flamen

Donn Piatt was a writer, editor, diplomat, humorist and gadfly of national reputation. *Library of Congress.*

Ball represented Fanny, while W.Y. Gholson and Chambers represented the claimants. The judge told them he would hear one argument from each side. After Mathews and Gholson rested their case, Warden said he would give his decision the following morning. "At this moment the woman Fanny stepped forward to the judge and said, 'I want to go home with my master, I can't fool away all dis time.'" Judge Warden instructed her to go, and she did.

The courtroom was filled with a respectful audience composed of both Black and white onlookers. No one made any attempt to deter the woman from leaving with Hutchinson. However, the *Cincinnati Nonpareil* reported, "Fanny was much frightened at the crowd, and the very cruel manner in which she had been treated."[184] Furthermore, "a gang of officers surrounded the poor creature, bawling in her ears, 'Tell the judge you want to go home with your master; say you want to go with him,'" etc., prompting her to change her mind.

The newspaper concluded, "We are no abolitionists, in the common acceptation of the term, but when our police officers show such slavish servility, and the knees of our judges knock together upon the bench, it is time for a press that claims to be independent, to speak out for justice and humanity."[185]

# 7

# THIS HOME OF THE FREE

*Oh, goodly and grand is our hunting to see,*
*In this "land of the brave and this home of the free."*
*—John Greenleaf Whittier, "The Hunters of Men"*

D rawing on her observations and research while residing in Cincinnati, Harriet Beecher Stowe wrote *Uncle Tom's Cabin*, arguably the most important American novel of all time. Published in 1852, it helped galvanize the antislavery movement in the United States and set the stage for the Civil War. Stowe managed to put a human face—or faces—on slavery and made people care about her "colored" and colorful characters.[186] No one could forget Eliza's daring escape across the broken ice of the Ohio River, clutching her baby in her arms and leaving a trail of bloody footprints. From that moment, the debate became less about preserving the Union and more about putting an end to slavery. Even Lincoln came to realize he couldn't do one without the other.

In 1849, George Washington "Wash" McQuerry and three other enslaved persons escaped from their owner, Henry Miller, some fifty miles outside of Louisville, Kentucky. Although one of his companions was soon apprehended, McQuerry and the other two crossed the Ohio River in a skiff at night, using pieces of bark as paddles. Making his way to Troy, Ohio, McQuerry settled down, married a free Black woman and fathered several children. In time, he came to be accepted and even respected as a member of the community.

Rumors that McQuerry was an escaped slave, however, reached a man named John Russell, who lived near the neighboring town of Piqua. Hoping to obtain a $1,000 reward, Russell wrote to Miller, notifying him where his missing slave could be found. With the help of four Kentuckians and a law officer, Miller undertook a search for McQuerry. They discovered that he was working on a canal boat. Placing him under arrest, they conveyed him to Dayton, where they turned him over to U.S. Deputy Marshal James M. Trader.

Harriet Beecher Stowe's *Uncle Tom's Cabin* became the best-selling novel of the nineteenth century. *Library of Congress.*

Although Miller had obtained a writ in the name of Sheriff Ebenezer Henderson of Montgomery County, the probate court judge who heard the case decided to leave McQuerry in Trader's custody. The party then continued on to Cincinnati, arriving at the Gait House on August 15, 1853.

Having heard a fugitive slave had been apprehended, a large crowd of African Americans began to gather. While they were quite vociferous in their sympathies for McQuerry, they did not challenge the local police who were brought in to keep order. But a free man of color named Peter H. Clerk immediately applied for a writ of habeas corpus from Justice John McLean of the Circuit Court who was staying nearby in Clifton. The paperwork, asking that he hear the case, reached McLean at two o'clock in the morning. "The writ was granted and made returnable about ten o'clock in the morning," according to historian Charles Greve.[187]

Miller then made application to U.S. Commissioner Samuel Carpenter who set the hearing for seven o'clock that same morning. When McQuerry was brought before him in irons, Carpenter ordered them removed. But because this was the first case to be adjudicated under the new Fugitive Slave Law, Carpenter preferred that it be heard by McLean.[188] So he postponed the hearing until two o'clock, "at the Criminal Court-room, until which time he had committed [the prisoner] to jail."[189]

When ten o'clock rolled around, Deputy Marshal Black, to whom a writ had been issued, notified Justice McLean that he did not have custody of McQuerry. Deputy Trader did. It wasn't until two o'clock that Marshals Black and Trader jointly hauled the prisoner before him. A huge crowd,

Many immigrants, including people of color, found work on the Miami-Erie Canal. *Authors' collection.*

of both Black and white spectators, had pressed into the courtroom and the jury box was occupied by women. Mayor David T. Snelbaker, who was also in attendance, had stationed large numbers of police in the immediate neighborhood in reaction to the public mood.

Miller was represented by T.C. Ware and McQuerry by John J. Jolliffe and James Birney. According to Grieve, the defendant "was a bright, well built and intelligent mulatto about 28 years old."[190] Upon his capture at Troy, Miller testified that "Wash," as he called him, said "nothing about being free, but observed that he had no intention to run off an hour before he started; that he was persuaded to do so by Steve, one of the individuals who accompanied him."[191] Both Trader and Black testified that McQuerry claimed that Miller was his master and that he had never been mistreated.

Despite not having a legal leg to stand on, Jolliffe

*delivered a long and impassioned argument upon the iniquity of the process by which an intelligent and upright human being who had lived for four years a sober, industrious and respected citizen of the State of Ohio could be dragged from his home and the wife of his bosom, from the graves of his children and bound hand and foot, hurried forever away from them and from all that he held dear into a bondage by the side of which Egyptian thralldom was a mercy.*[192]

Jolliffe also insisted that the Fugitive Slave Law was unconstitutional, especially since it did not permit a trial by jury. However, that was a matter for a higher court to decide.

After reviewing the evidence and the law, McLean declared in the case of *Miller v. McQuerry*: "This is not a case for sympathy....Let those who think differently go to the people who make the laws. I cannot turn aside from the sacred duties of my office to regard aught by the law....I am bound to *remand the fugitive to his master*."[193] He specifically referred to *Prigg v. Pennsylvania*.

The prisoner was handed over to the marshal and taken to Covington, Kentucky. While Miller was willing to sell McQuerry to those who wanted to buy his freedom, not enough money could be raised. Consequently, McQuerry "disappeared from history into the darkness of Southern slavedom."[194]

Some freedom seekers were prepared to fend off slave catchers. *Authors' collection.*

Ten days later, on August 25, 1853, three unrelated slaves—Hannah, Edward and Susan—were removed from the steamboat *Tropic* at Cincinnati and taken before Judge Jacob Flinn on a writ of habeas corpus initiated by Reverend William Troy, a free Black man.[195] Upon being alerted to the situation, Troy had immediately gone down to the dock, boarded the vessel and confirmed it was true.

"Knowing that according to the State law," Troy wrote, "these persons were illegally detained, I proceeded at once to take steps to release them. My lawyer made out an affidavit, which was acknowledged by a notary public, and with it I went to see one of the judges, with whom I was acquainted; but, unfortunately for me and the work in which I was engaged, he was not at home."[196]

Troy then went in search of his second choice but could not find him, either. Fearing the boat would soon be leaving, he reluctantly sought out Judge Flinn. An Irishman, Jacob Flinn was known to be a strong pro-slavery Democrat. Nevertheless, he agreed to sign the document, and Troy and the sheriff rushed to the steamer with it. On the strength of the affidavit, they conveyed the trio to the courthouse for a hearing before Flinn. The slaves were the property of Lemuel Doty and James Ambrose and had been entrusted to their agent, Lemuel Lipsey. It was likely they were being transported from western Virginia to the Southern slave markets.

Troy's counsel—John Jolliffe—was present, as was counsel secured by the master of the slaves. Jolliffe asserted that by the very act of having been brought onto free soil, the three enslaved persons were legally free according to the laws of Ohio. The opposing counsel argued that the owner had the right to take the slaves wherever he pleased, just as he would a horse or a mule.

Because Hannah, an elderly woman, said she wanted to return to her master, Flinn ordered her into the custody of the claimant without further investigation. He then asked Hannah if she had custody of the child, Susan, who appeared to be four or five years old. When she acknowledged that she did, the judge ordered Susan back to the claimant as well. Although Jolliffe protested, the court said it would take responsibility.

That left Edward, age eighteen.

"It appeared that [the slaves] were purchased in Virginia, to be conveyed to Mississippi. The boat stopped at Cincinnati, and the slaves were twice taken by the agent of the owners on shore, and upon the territory of Ohio," the *Cincinnati Gazette* reported.[197] They had originally intended to dock at Covington, Kentucky, but low water forced them to stop at Cincinnati.

Before he could finish presenting his case, Jolliffe was taken ill and had to leave the courtroom. Although he begged for an adjournment until the next morning, Judge Flinn refused. "The case will he decided to-night; that is decided on," Flinn said. "We have not been sitting here four or five hours to determine whether we will decide the case or not. It will be decided, and you may come up to it sideways or square; or any way you please; you must come to it."[198]

Agitated beyond reason, Flinn then declared, "I will bring this to an end," and had the courtroom cleared.[199] It was his opinion that the owner of the slaves had not intended for them to step foot in Ohio, so he ordered the sheriff to take the slaves across the Ohio River and deliver them to their master.

Troy was saddened by the spectacle of seeing Edward and the others escorted from the courthouse. But Judge Flinn was not finished. A week or so later, Flinn encountered Jolliffe on the street and promptly knocked him down without provocation other than his disagreement with his politics. Flinn was the first elected judge of the newly created Criminal Court in Hamilton County. However, he behaved so disgracefully that the court was abolished two years later simply to get rid of him.

Sometimes the courtroom itself, rather than the judgment, was the vehicle for a slave's freedom. Lewis (or possibly Louis) Williams was, legally speaking, the property of Alexander Marshall of Flemington, Kentucky. In June 1850, just three months before the passage of the Fugitive Slave Act, sixteen-year-old Lewis fled from his master's home. Deputy Marshal James Black tracked him as far as Cincinnati before losing him. Lewis purportedly received assistance in his flight from some agents of the Underground Railroad. When he reached Columbus, he settled down as a free man for the next three years.

Then on October 15, 1853, U.S. Marshal Manuel Dryden captured Lewis about ten miles north of Columbus. When local abolitionists learned that Dryden planned to transport Lewis back to Kentucky, they sent a telegram to attorney John Jolliffe in Cincinnati. Jolliffe sprang into action, "claiming the negro was not a slave."[200] The following day, as Dryden arrived at the Railroad Depot in Cincinnati with Lewis in tow, the federal marshal was placed under arrest on the charge of kidnapping a free man.

The contrasting appearance of the hunter and the hunted was captured by a reporter for the *Cincinnati Columbian*. Dryden was described as "a well enough but carelessly dressed man, long nose, obstinate mouth, one trousers leg above his boots, and his hair standing straight up and straight back—perhaps he had not had time to arrange it, since his vigorous pursuit of the fugitive."[201]

Lewis, on the other hand, was "a yellow boy, of say nineteen years of age; thick, curly hair, and a broad nose; otherwise his features are not those of the negro; check shirt, large plaid trousers in the latest fashion, and a mixed overcoat lined with red plaid, and the sleeves turned up at the wrists to display the gay lining."[202]

Dryden asked for a federal commissioner to determine whether Lewis was a slave. If the commissioner agreed that he was, then the kidnapping charges against Dryden would be dropped. U.S. Commissioner Samuel Carpenter scheduled the hearing for the very next day, Monday, October 17, in Wilson's Building on Court Street. The new courthouse was still under construction, replacing one that had been largely consumed in a fire four years earlier.[203]

Jolliffe and another young attorney, Rutherford B. Hayes, were lined up in Lewis's corner.[204] "They endeavored to prove that Louis [*sic*] had formerly accompanied his master to this State to aid him in driving a drove of horses back to Kentucky, and that under the law of Ohio, which liberated every slave who came into the State by his master's consent, Louis was free."[205] The hearing was postponed, however, to allow the slaveholder to return home to gather evidence and secure witnesses.

When the hearing resumed, Dryden presented two witnesses—Francis T. Chambers and A.S. Sullivan—who claimed to have known Lewis as a slave. He also produced an affidavit from his owner, Alexander Marshall. The trial lasted for several days; there was enormous interest in the case, and the courtroom was packed with spectators, both white and Black.

However, Carpenter resisted pressure to make a quick ruling. He took time to review the documents and testimony, although there was ample evidence to return the young man to slavery at once. Supposedly, Carpenter was intimidated by the crowd and spoke in whispers, which required those in attendance to listen very attentively. "After hearing the evidence, he deferred making his judgment until the next day."[206]

The *Cincinnati Gazette* reported that at half past two in the afternoon on October

Before becoming president of the United States, Rutherford B. Hayes defended many runaway slaves. *Library of Congress.*

20, 1853, Lewis Williams was brought before Carpenter for his decision. But an application was made for continuance on the grounds that new testimony had come to light in a telegraph message from Judge Spalding in Columbus. Spalding also expressed the desire to hear the case in his own Circuit Court.

While Carpenter was in the process of conveying his decision to grant the motion, Lewis, who had been sitting with Marshal Dryden, pushed his chair back, ostensibly to gain some leg room. He then slid it back some more, quietly stood up and took a step back. "A friend put a good hat on his head," historian Charles Greve would later write,

> and he moved cautiously toward a part of the room where the colored people were gathered. A number of the abolitionists watched his every movement with anxious fear lest he should be discovered. At the door a passageway was made for him and he passed into the street, through an alley, crossed the canal through the German settlement and stole by an indirect route to Avondale, where he knew the sexton of the colored burying ground.[207]

Realizing Lewis was gone, Dryden "started in pursuit—the crowded audience cheering as he left the Court room."[208] Oddly, the *Cincinnati Gazette* reported that the arrest had been kept quiet, there was little excitement about the case and Commissioner Carpenter had remanded Lewis back to his master.[209]

Years later, William Troy and Levi Coffin wrote about the incident, although their memories of it do not always coincide. Born in Essex County, Virginia, in 1827, Troy was the son of a free Black woman who had purchased her husband's freedom. After being baptized into the Baptist church, he was dismayed to hear the church pastor delivering sermons to justify his and the deacon's personal trade in slaves, including members of their own congregation. Finally, Reverend Troy and his wife moved to Cincinnati in 1848.

Despite going into considerable detail, Troy seems to have conflated Cincinnati and Columbus. He wrote that when Lewis fled Kentucky, he stopped in Cincinnati for several years, staying with a friend just outside the city limits. There he fell in love with a local girl. But because he was uncertain of her feelings for him, he consulted with a Dutch woman who was known as a fortune-teller. After paying her the equivalent of one dollar in silver, Lewis revealed to her he was a fugitive from Kentucky. He also told her the name of his master and the master's post office address.

Levi and Catherine Coffin worked together to assist many fugitives in their flight to freedom. *Authors' collection.*

The fortune-teller told the lovestruck young man that not only would he meet with success, but that the girl loved him and they would marry within three months. Naturally, Lewis was encouraged by this prediction and departed as a satisfied customer. But the woman wasn't done. She immediately shared with her husband what she had learned about the escaped slave. They then wrote a letter to Alexander Marshall, promising to tell him where Lewis was if he paid them $200. Accepting their proposal, he came to Cincinnati and paid them the money, and they told him where he could locate Lewis. Shortly after that, Lewis was arrested by Marshal Dryden.

It was at this point that Reverend Troy first became involved. Having heard news of the incident, Troy met with the marshals who had custody of Lewis to learn what had occurred. He then went directly to see John Jolliffe, knowing that the attorney handled such cases for free. While Jolliffe went to the courthouse to arrange to be Lewis's counsel, Troy claimed that he went to "spread the news among the coloured people of the city, in order that some plan might be devised to get the boy out of the court house, if possible. We became a sort of committee of ways and means."[210]

Troy related that they devised a plan to pack the courtroom and somehow free Lewis. Levi Coffin was present as well, and he recalled the scene:

> *The room was long and had a table or counter through the center. On the west side of this there was a crowd of colored people, standing; the judge and lawyers were sitting at the table. Opposite them sat the slave, between his master and the marshal of Columbus, and just behind him stood a crowd of white people, composed of friends of the slave, and others who had been drawn to the spot by matters of curiosity.*[211]

According to Troy, they had arranged to temporarily replace Lewis with a man who had a similar complexion. As soon as the man placed his hat on Lewis's head, Lewis slowly rose from his chair and the substitute sat down in it. "The attention of the marshal at this time was attracted by certain points in dispute between the counsel, and the prisoner by this time had made his way through the great crowd, on his hands and knees, to the door, and out he slipped and made to the forest."[212]

Coffin added that Lewis passed through a throng of Germans to the street where he "made his way quickly, though with not enough haste to attract attention, through an alley, across the canal, through the German settlement, and by an indirect route to Avondale, where he knew the sexton of the colored burying ground."[213]

It wasn't until after the dispute was resolved that Dryden noticed that his prisoner was missing and exclaimed, "Where is the boy?" A person who was standing at the door responded, "The child left some time ago; no use to look, for the creature is going to the Queen; he don't like this country."[214] The marshal made a mad dash for the door, followed by supporters of the fugitive slave. With Dryden's departure, the reading of Commissioner Carpenter's opinion was suspended.

The following night, the conspirators brought Lewis back from the forest and into the city, where they lodged him in Troy's house, which was on Broadway near Sixth Street. Although Troy knew that harboring a fugitive slave was a violation of federal law and he could be imprisoned for six months and fine $1,000, his courage was sustained by the belief that his actions were favored by God.

Lewis remained for about a week hidden in an upper room. Only two or three people knew he was being secreted there, but the residence was in a busy neighborhood so the abolitionists decided they should hide him elsewhere. One night, Troy moved him to his office, also on Broadway.

On the following Sunday morning, Troy was sitting in the pulpit of a church, awaiting his turn to preach, when a friend signaled him that there was a problem. Excusing himself, he went outside the chapel, where he was informed that police officers had his office under surveillance.

Troy quickly arranged to obtain some articles of women's attire—dresses and skirts, bonnet and a veil, including a "whopping crinoline"—from a friend's daughter. But when he tried to dress Lewis in the garments, he found that he did not possess the necessary skills. So he asked two of his female friends to perform the task, and they were happy to oblige. After they were finished, they had Lewis parade back and forth before them until they were satisfied that he could imitate their manner of walking.[215]

Satisfied with Lewis's disguise, Troy then asked his eldest brother to take "this supposed lady" to the chapel that afternoon. "They both walked out of the door of the business place, through the back yard, and passed through the crowd of policemen, apparently unnoticed. They made their way down Broadway, the veil, bonnet, and crinoline adding much to the appearance of the supposed lady."[216]

Once more dressed in women's apparel, Lewis walked down Broadway one Sunday evening to the corner of Eighth Street, where he then followed Coffin through a side gate and into the basement of a Congregational church. Here, he was hidden away in a committee room for several more weeks while the search for him went on. Dryden disguised himself as a Quaker and, using an alias, visited several settlements of the Society of Friends, asking about Lewis. But they told him nothing.

To further mislead Lewis's pursuers, a telegram was sent to Cincinnati from Columbus and published in the *Gazette*, claiming that Lewis had passed through the city on a train bound for Cleveland. Another telegram from Cleveland said he had boarded a boat for Detroit. All the time, Lewis was residing in the church. Finally, a Presbyterian minister and his wife who were visiting Cincinnati offered to drive him out of the city in their carriage.

As Coffin wrote, "Louis, disguised as a woman with a veil over his face, entered the carriage and sat on the back seat by the lady. They took him about thirty miles out of the city, that day, to a noted depot of the Underground Railroad, and he was duly shipped to Sandusky, where he arrived in safety and took the boat for Canada."[217]

Alternately, Lewis made his way to Cleveland, where he walked into the office of William Howard Day, who put him on a steamer to Canada. He may have settled in Malden, where he lived as William Alexander. Since neither Troy nor Coffin accompanied him, it is not surprising that their accounts diverge slightly.

Afterward, an article appeared in a Cincinnati newspaper excoriating the church for having hidden the fugitive. "What is to become of the rights of slaveholders, and the divinely appointed institution [of slavery]," the writer asked, "if ministers will connive at such plans to defraud owners of their property?"[218]

Under the Fugitive Slave Act, Marshal Dryden was personally liable to the slave owner for the loss of his property. Although he used every means at his disposal to recapture Lewis, Dryden failed to do so. In the end, he owed Alexander Marshall the sum of $1,000, but the slave owner settled for $800.

Coffin claimed that Carpenter later "told him that he expected to decide that the Fugitive Slave Law conferred on him, as commissioner, judicial powers which he could not constitutionally exercise."[219] A year later, Carpenter, as well as U.S. Commissioner P.B. Wilcox of Columbus, announced that they would "hereafter refuse to do that kind of dirty work."[220]

# 8

# RIGHT MERRILY HUNTING

*Right merrily hunting the black man, whose sin*
*Is the curl of his hair and the hue of his skin!*
—*John Greenleaf Whittier, "The Hunters of Men"*

Aletter published in the *Marysville Eagle* in November 1852 expressed the frustrations and concerns of one would-be slave catcher. He had just completed a trip through Ohio to Canada in pursuit of runaways. During the few days he stopped in Sandusky, "upwards of thirty fugitives crossed the Lake."[221] He learned from the captain of a steamer that regularly traveled between Sandusky and Detroit that "in the last two months over two hundred had crossed from the State of Kentucky alone."[222] Of some seventy enslaved individuals who had escaped from Kentucky recently, only three had been retaken.

The manhunter's fellow passengers on the vessel included several escapees. He introduced himself to one of them who was from Louisville. The "property" of a Mr. Ford of Owenton, he had stolen a boat and paddled across the Ohio River. He then made his way to Cincinnati, where he boarded a train for Sandusky.

Believing that slaves were generally "pretty well satisfied," the Kentuckian asked "the boy" what had induced him to run away.[223] He replied that "it was 'wrong to serve a master' and that the 'reading negroes told him that it was against the Bible.' He further stated that next summer there would an awful lumbering of the darkies to the free grounds."[224] Many slave owners did view literacy as a threat.

THE GREAT AMERICAN BUCK HUNT OF 1856.

The Kansas-Nebraska Act resulted in open warfare between pro- and anti-slavery factions. *Library of Congress.*

Upon docking in Canada, the Kentuckian heard the same thing from others. He concluded his letter with the following advice to his fellow slave hunters:

> *In pursuing fugitives at present, I find two leading difficulties to contend with, one is to get the right kind of men to follow them without paying their expenses independent of the reward, the other is, to avoid indiscreet persons who only follow a day or two in a kind of boisterous frolic—who abuse every person they come across, whether abolitionist or not, and not unfrequently threatened to burn every town in their view.*[225]

The runaway problem had become so concerning that slaveholders in Mason and Bracken Counties met at Minerva, Kentucky, on November 16, 1852, to implement steps to secure their slaves. As the *Republic*, a Washington, D.C. newspaper summed it up: "The slaveholders have good reason to fear that Kentucky will shortly become a free State, for the simple reason that their slaves won't stay."[226]

On May 30, 1854, the antislavery clause of the Missouri Compromise was negated by the passage of the Kansas-Nebraska Act. Authored by

Lincoln's political opponent Stephen A. Douglas was known as "The Little Giant." *Library of Congress.*

Senator Stephen A. Douglas of Illinois, it allowed the two new territories to choose whether they wanted to be slave or free.[227] This resulted in the split of the Whig Party. The Southern Whigs joined the pro-slavery Democrats while the Northern Whigs united with other antislavery factions to form the Republican Party. Soon, the territories erupted in violence; in Ohio, the struggle over slavery continued to intensify.

Nine slaves made a break for freedom on Sunday, June 11, 1854. They were Shadrack, age sixty; his wife, Susan, twenty-nine; their two boys, Wesley and John, nine and seven; Lee, twenty-one; his wife, Almeda, twenty-six; and her child, Sarah Jane, three; Lewis, twenty-four; and Anderson, twenty-two. The fugitives were owned by William Walton, John Gaines (as guardian of Elizabeth Ann and Jasper Blackenbecker), John P. Scott and Jonas Crisler.

Leaving Burlington, Boone County, Kentucky, the fugitives took three horses with them, presumably for use by the children. When they reached the river, they turned the horses loose and crossed to the Ohio side at midnight in a skiff. They continued on for two or three miles before hiding themselves in the bush. There they remained throughout the next day, emerging only after dark when they resumed walking north.

A Black man named John Gyser happened upon them and offered his assistance. Taking them to a stable near Lick Run, he told them to remain there until nightfall. But he had no intention of helping them. He went directly to Covington, Kentucky, learned that a $1,000 reward had been offered for their apprehension and betrayed their location to some slave catchers.

That evening, a posse led by U.S. Deputy Marshal George Thayer, Deputy City Marshals Lee and Worley and Sheriff Ward of Covington surrounded the stable. One of the slaves was playing a violin as the posse rushed in. They quickly took the fugitives prisoner, arresting them on a warrant issued by U.S. Commissioner John L. Pendery on the oath of William Walton.[228] Placed in handcuffs, they were transported to Cincinnati, where they appeared before Commissioner Pendery.

Representing the Kentuckians were attorneys George H. Ketchum, George E. Pugh and someone named Dudley, while the runaways were defended by John Jolliffe and John Getchell. All were from Cincinnati save Dudley of Covington. Pugh would become a U.S. senator in 1855.

According to the *New York Herald*, Shadrack was a "veritable 'Uncle Tom,'" dressed in pants made from the same cloth as his master's clothes.[229] Crisler, his owner, praised him for his high character and believed he ran away only because he was induced to do so by white men. A parade of witnesses testified on behalf of the slaveholders, confirming they knew the fugitives in their capacity as slaves. "The negroes did not complain of ill treatment," the *New York Herald* reported, "but…Shadrach [*sic*] stated that they had runaway because they had been told that they were going to be sold down the river."[230]

In rendering his decision, Pendery pointed out that the constitutionality of slavery had been upheld by the highest court in the land, the identity of the persons had been proven and the defendants were found to owe service to their respective claimants. Consequently, all nine of them were remanded to their owners. Crisler, for one, said he did not want to take Shadrack back and would sell him for a pittance. He had "always been an excellent slave, but now he didn't want him."[231]

Surrounded by a bevy of police officers and special deputy marshals, the prisoners were placed aboard an omnibus and driven to the Walnut Street ferry landing with some eight hundred people following behind. From there, they were taken across the river to Covington and lodged in the jail before being returned to slavery.

On June 20, 1854, a letter from Commissioner Carpenter was published in the *Cincinnati Gazette* in which he refuted the constitutionality of the portion of the Fugitive Slave Act that required commissioners to issue warrants and hear cases. He asserted that he would continue to refuse to issue warrants. Among commissioners, anyway, his was a lone voice.

Coming ten years after the Jerry Finney decision, the Rosetta Armstead (occasionally Armistead) affair once again pitted Ohio against Kentucky in a court battle that was even more contentious. But this time there was a happy ending. Rosetta—"about sixteen years of age, small size, rather corpulent, and a dark mulatto"—was the legal property of Reverend Henry M. Dennison, the rector of St. Paul's Episcopal Church in Louisville, Kentucky.[232] Born in

President John Tyler was a slave owner, yet he believed slavery was innately evil. *Library of Congress*.

Pennsylvania, Henry had married Alice Tyler, a young woman from Virginia, who was the daughter of former United States president John Tyler.

As a wedding gift, Tyler gave his daughter Rosetta to wait on her. He owned about four dozen slaves at the time. Four years after the couple settled in Louisville, Alice Tyler Dennison died on June 8, 1854, leaving an infant child. Later that month, Henry delivered his young daughter to Virginia to stay with her mother's relatives. A couple of months after that, he decided to send Rosetta to them as well to attend to the baby. He asked Dr. Jones Miller, a friend, to accompany her.

In March 1855, Dr. Miller set off with Rosetta on a steamboat. His intent was to take her to Wheeling, [West] Virginia, and then onto Richmond, Virginia, never stepping foot in a free state. But when they reached Cincinnati, the river became impassable due to ice and they were forced to disembark. They then boarded a train.

Dr. Miller planned "to cross the State of Ohio by the Little Miami Railway to Columbus and thence by the Central Ohio Railway through Zanesville to Wheeling," according to historian Alfred Lee.[233] Once they were underway, however, he learned there would be a stopover in Zanesville on Sunday. Apprehensive that he might experience some trouble from abolitionists in the adjoining town of Putnam, Miller decided to remain in Columbus overnight.

While en route, Rosetta struck up a conversation with another Black passenger. Learning that she was a slave, the stranger informed her that she was entitled to her freedom because she had been brought into Ohio by consent of her master. When the train reached Columbus, the man immediately notified his friends about her situation. Some of them followed Miller and the girl to where they were spending the night, likely the home of his brother, John G. Miller. During the next few hours, several African American women somehow communicated with Rosetta, and she repeated her desire to be free.

The Reverend William B. Ferguson, a Baptist minister, engaged an attorney to procure a writ of habeas corpus on her behalf. The first judge who was approached refused to do so, but the second, Probate Judge William Jamison (some sources say Supreme Court Judge Joseph R. Swan), was agreeable.

"Sheriff Miller, at near midnight, rapped at the door of the house where the girl was held, and after considerable parlay and delay, came forth with the girl, and took her to prison for safekeeping until the hour for the meeting of the court on Monday" the *Anti-Slavery Bugle* recounted.[234] At the appointed time, Rosetta appeared in court.

"Rosetta is a smart, intelligent girl, and appears to appreciate fully the benefits of freedom," one reporter noted.[235] And it was generally conceded that she was entitled to it if she wanted it. The courtroom was packed with many people of color, and the girl was nearly overwhelmed by the reception she received from them. "We rejoice always at the rescue of a human being from the prison-house of bondage."[236] Since she was a minor, however, she needed to be placed under the charge of a guardian. At the suggestion of her counsel, she chose Louis G. Van Slyke, who posted bond and took her home.

Not long afterward, Reverend Dennison arrived in Columbus and met with Rosetta at the Van Slyke residence. He told her he had come to take her home if she wished to go. She replied that she would prefer to remain in a free state rather than return to slavery. Dennison then shook hands with Rosetta and departed, "evidently much grieved at the loss of a favorite servant."[237] The girl was subsequently employed by Dr. James H. Coulter.

However, Rosetta's freedom proved to be short-lived. Dennison took his case to Commissioner John Pendery in Cincinnati, who had previously asserted that the constitutionality of slavery had been upheld in the United States Supreme Court. The commissioner issued a warrant for her arrest. On March 23, 1855, two weeks after she was granted her freedom in Columbus, Rosetta was at Dr. Coulter's house when Marshal Bennet and ex-officer Couch paid a visit. Apparently, they were in the employ of U.S.

Deputy Marshal Hiram H. Robinson. They asked to see the doctor, but he was not home. Spotting Rosetta, they placed her under arrest.

Marshal Robinson then transported her by train to Cincinnati, where she was lodged in jail. Her arrest led to angry demonstrations by a mob of people, both white and Black, and threats to rescue her. Fortunately, Van Slyke had managed to board the same train. Before Rosetta could be brought before Pendery, he obtained a writ of habeas corpus. A legal team that included Salmon P. Chase, future governor of Ohio, and Rutherford B. Hayes, future president of the United States, was assembled. The case was heard by Judge Parker.

"After extended argument by counsel," historian Alfred Lee related, "Judge Parker held that as Rosetta had been brought from Kentucky into Ohio by her master or his agent she was free and should be delivered to the custody of Mr. Van Slyke, her guardian."[238]

But Dennison wasn't through. He went back to Pendery and filed an affidavit accusing the girl of being a fugitive from labor and service. This time, he ensured that Pendery would hear the case. So as soon as Rosetta was released from custody, she was rearrested by Marshal Robinson on the same warrant he had used previously. When notified what had transpired, Judge Parker issued a summons to Robinson for contempt of court. The marshal refused to obey, and he was fined fifty dollars and imprisoned.

Finally brought before Commissioner Pendery, Rosetta likely expected the worst. But "the Commissioner decided that the claimant, Dennison, was bound by the act of his agent Miller; that there was no escape on Rosetta's part; that bringing her to Columbus and there offering her freedom was equivalent to emancipating her. He then declared Rosetta free."[239] Apparently, Pendery's views were evolving.

Rosetta "Anderson" (as she was identified in the court records) was released to popular acclaim, at least on the Ohio side of the river. In Kentucky, there were a series of meetings by the state's most influential slaveholders, railing against the actions of the courts of Ohio and other northern states. Concerned about the impact on their property rights, they were highly critical of Dennison for not fighting harder to retain custody of the girl.

With five hundred well-wishers gathered at the depot to see them off, Van Slyke took charge of Rosetta, and they boarded a train for Columbus. Dennison would subsequently file suit to recover the monetary loss of Rosetta. He was countersued for $10,000 for malicious prosecution and false imprisonment on behalf of the girl.[240]

John Jolliffe sought to defend Margaret Garner by having her charged with murder.
*Authors' collection.*

As for Rosetta, she soon started on a journey to New England, courtesy of a wealthy woman from there who happened to be in Columbus at the time. She had taken a special interest "in her welfare, and, upon her being declared free by the laws of Ohio, agreed, with the consent of the girl's friends, to take her home, and have her educated at her expense, in one of the best seminaries in the land."[241]

And "for his arduous efforts in obtaining the girl's rescue from slavery, the colored people of Columbus" presented Van Slyke with a silver pitcher at a ceremony held at city hall, much like those in Cincinnati had previously done for Salmon Chase.[242]

One of the most famous and heartbreaking fugitive slave incidents occurred early the following year during one of the coldest winters on record. On the night of January 27, 1856, a party of slaves—perhaps as many as seventeen—fled from Boone County, Kentucky. After crossing the ice-encrusted Ohio River, they split up, with some hiding out in the home of Joe Kite, a free Black man, not far from Cincinnati. Among the fugitives was Margaret Garner; her husband, Robert (sometimes referred to as Simon Jr.); their four children; and Robert's parents, Simon and Mary.

Unsure what to do with them, Kite, who was Margaret's uncle, hurried uptown to confer with Levi Coffin at his store. Coffin and his wife, Catherine, were already so well known for their Underground Railroad work that Harriet Beecher Stowe had modeled the characters of Simeon and Rachel Halliday in *Uncle Tom's Cabin* after them. Coffin advised him to relocate them to a Black settlement farther up Millcreek. However, a posse of slave catchers was in close pursuit and had heard that a group of Black people had been asking directions to Kite's residence.

The next morning, the posse arrived at the house with an arrest warrant issued by Commissioner Pendery. They were accompanied by U.S. Deputy Marshal John Ellis and a band of officers. Unable to flee, the "escaped slaves prepared to battle for freedom and barred the windows and doors, refusing admittance to the officers of the law," historian Charles Greve wrote.[243]

Margaret, known as "Peggy," was born on Maplewood plantation and was owned by John Pollard Gaines. She was biracial, and there is some suggestion that she may have been John's daughter. In 1849, she married Robert Garner, an enslaved man owned by a neighbor, John Marshall. Before the year was out, the plantation was sold to her master's younger brother, Archibald K. Gaines, after John was appointed governor of the Oregon Territory by President Zachary Taylor.

Three of Margaret's subsequent children were described as "mullatoes [*sic*]" and very likely were fathered by "the Colonel," Archibald Gaines, said to be a much more brutal and cruel master than his brother. There is little reason to doubt that Margaret was abused and probably raped. When Levi Coffin later asked her about a scar on the left side of her forehead and cheeks, she answered frankly, "White man struck me."[244]

As the posse, which included Gaines and John Marshall's son, battered down a window and rushed into Kite's house, Robert, Margaret's husband, fired four shots with a six-shooter before he was overpowered. In desperation, Margaret seized a butcher knife and warned the men that she would kill all of her children rather than permit them to be carried back to slavery. Before the slave hunters could stop her, the pregnant and half-mad woman had nearly beheaded her youngest child, a two- or three-year-old girl named Mary. She also made an attempt to kill the others as well as herself.

All of the fugitives save for the dead girl were conveyed to the police station. Their friends obtained a writ of habeas corpus the same day, requiring the county sheriff to take the slaves into custody and confine them in the country jail—thus setting up a legal showdown. The probate judge quickly hopped a train to Columbus in order to confer with Governor Salmon Chase. Newly elected, Chase had taken office just fourteen days before. The judge obtained the governor's assurance "that the process of the State courts should be enforced in every part of the State, and that the sheriff would be sustained in the performance of his duty by the whole power at the command of the executive."[245]

In the trial before Commissioner Pendery, defense attorneys John Jolliffe and John W. Getchell argued that Margaret, Robert and Mary Garner had previously been emancipated by having been in Ohio with their master's consent. In an affidavit, Margaret swore that she had been "brought to Cincinnati to nurse Mary Gaines, daughter of the said John Gaines, who now lives with her uncle, Archibald Gaines, in Kentucky that she came here in the morning and went back on the evening of the said day."[246] Her children William, Samuel and Miller were all born after that time. Robert and Mary told similar stories in their affidavits.

Pendery, however, said he was obligated to remand them to their owners because the slaves had not asserted their freedom on those occasions when they had previously visited Ohio.

Switching tactics, Jolliffe then declared that Margaret should be tried for murder. Colonel Francis T. Chambers of Cincinnati, attorney for the slave owners, objected: "The practical effect of all these sort of motions was to abolish the Fugitive Slave Law at once. All a fugitive would have to do would be to commit some trifling offense, and he would become the prisoner of the State of Ohio."[247]

Jolliffe's plan was to prevent Margaret from being carried back into slavery by trying her and the other adults for the slaying of little Mary. Even if convicted, they would be better off in an Ohio prison—with the prospect of parole—than enslaved for the rest of their lives. "The fugitives have all assured me," Jolliffe said, "that they will go singing to the gallows rather than be returned to slavery."[248] Nevertheless, Gaines promised the court he would bring Margaret back to Ohio to stand trial if the murder charge was pressed.

On February 8, 1856, the grand jury indicted the parents and the grandparents of the slain child for murder. Furthermore, the probate judge issued a writ of habeas corpus for the three surviving children and made a special order preventing them from being removed from his jurisdiction pending his decision in the murder case.

At the same time, the U.S. marshal applied to U.S. District Court Judge Humphrey Leavitt for a writ of habeas corpus to determine whether the sheriff was entitled to the custody of the four fugitives "under the criminal process of the State, rather than the marshal under the Slave Act commissioner's warrant."[249]

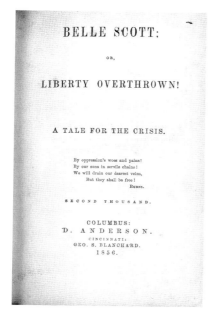

BELLE SCOTT;

OR,

LIBERTY OVERTHROWN!

A TALE FOR THE CRISIS.

By oppression's woes and pains!
By our sons in servile chains!
We will drain our dearest veins,
But they shall be free!
BURNS.

SECOND THOUSAND.

COLUMBUS:
D. ANDERSON.
CINCINNATI:
GEO. S. BLANCHARD.
1856.

Inspired by the Margaret Garner affair, John Jolliffe wrote the antislavery novel *Belle Scott*. *Authors' collection.*

To the surprise of nearly everyone, Judge Leavitt announced on February 28 that the sheriff should deliver the indicted individuals into the custody of the marshal. The sheriff not only complied but also gave the marshal custody of the three children.

"The fugitives were immediately hurried into an omnibus, guarded by a posse of five hundred special deputy marshals, driven to the river, and taken across on the ferry-boat to Kentucky," historian John Trowbridge noted.[250] It took less than an hour for them to be locked in a Kentucky jail.

Governor Chase was shocked by this turn of events.

"No one imagined that a judge could be found who would undertake to transfer, by a proceeding in *habeas corpus*, persons indicted under a State law to United States custody under the Fugitive-slave Act"—let alone that the children would be surrendered in violation of the order.[251]

Although Chase continued to seek the return of the Garner family to Ohio, it was too late. They were quickly sent away to the Deep South. According to the *Liberator*, the Garners were on board the steamboat *Henry Lewis* when it struck another boat and sank in March 1856. Margaret and a baby were pitched overboard. The child drowned, and Margaret allegedly tried to drown herself but failed. Still, she was said to be happy her baby was dead.

After briefly being held in Arkansas, the Garners were sent to New Orleans to work as household servants. When the *Cincinnati Chronicle* interviewed Robert Garner in 1870, he said they were sold to Judge Dewitt Clinton Bonham at Tennessee Landing, Mississippi, in 1857. A year later, Margaret died of typhoid fever.

The coda of the Garner affair occurred on June 1, 1857, when Archibald Gaines encountered John Jolliffe on the streets of Covington. After verbally abusing the attorney as a slave stealer, he raised a mob to physically assault him. If not for the intervention of the law, Jolliffe might well have been lynched. The year before, Jolliffe had published (anonymously) *Belle Scott, or Liberty Overthrown*, a novel inspired by the Garner case. Simultaneously, Harriet Beecher Stowe incorporated part of Garner's story in her novel *Dred: A Tale of the Great Dismal Swamp*. In 1987, Ohio author Toni Morrison published *Beloved*, also inspired by the story of Margaret Garner. A year later, it won the Pulitzer Prize for Fiction.

# 9

# AND WOMAN, KIND WOMAN

*And woman, kind woman, wife, widow, and maid,*
*For the good of the hunted, is lending her aid.*
—*John Greenleaf Whittier, "The Hunters of Men"*

F ive years before the outbreak of Civil War, the political rancor in Congress was so intense that when Senator Charles Sumner of Massachusetts gave a powerful speech on May 22, 1856, denouncing the Kansas-Nebraska Act, Senator Preston Brooks of South Carolina nearly beat him to death with a cane two days later on the floor of the chamber. For the next three years, Sumner's seat was left vacant while he struggled to recover from his injuries. When he did return, he was outspoken in his belief that the war had to be fought to end slavery and not just to save the Union. He remained an uncompromising champion of civil rights until the day he died.

In Ohio, dissatisfaction with the Fugitive Slave Act had been growing. Determined to address it, the Republican- dominated legislature enacted three personal liberty laws on April 17, 1857. First, the legislators made it a felony to hold a person as a slave within the boundaries of the state. Second, they prohibited holding a slave in any Ohio jail. And third, they mandated a sentence of three to eight years at hard labor in the Ohio Penitentiary for anyone who kidnapped or decoyed a Black or "mulatto" person out of the state without due process. However, it came to naught the following year when the Democrats took control of the legislature and

SOUTHERN CHIVALRY — ARGUMENT versus CLUB'S.

The caning of Charles Sumner by Preston Brooks was viewed as the "breakdown of reasoned discourse." *Library of Congress.*

repealed all laws regarding the kidnapping of free Black people and the use of Ohio jails to hold slaves.

Roger B. Taney started out to be an unlikely villain in the history of American slavery. Prior to becoming chief justice of the United States Supreme Court in 1836, Taney had sought to restrict slaveholding as a member of the Maryland senate. He had also freed eleven slaves he inherited when he was younger. And as the defense counsel for Reverend Jacob Gruber, an abolitionist preacher, he had denounced slavery as "a blot on our national character."[252] Yet his reputation as a jurist rests largely on his role in the Dred Scott decision.

Writing for the majority in *Dred Scott v. Sandford*, Taney's views had clearly shifted. A Jacksonian Democrat, he adamantly opposed any attempt by the federal government to meddle in matters that he believed were the purview of the states. His focus was on individual liberty—for white people, anyway—which he felt was threatened by the concentration of too much power in Washington. He viewed the issue of slavery as the wedge that was dividing the country, so he sought to take it off the table.

Originally from Missouri, Dred Scott was a slave who appealed to the Supreme Court to affirm his right to freedom. His argument was based on

The Dred Scott decision is widely regarded as the worst ever handed down by the U.S. Supreme Court. *Library of Congress.*

the grounds that his master, John Sanford (no "d"), had taken him to live for a time in Illinois, which was a free state, and then Wisconsin, which was a free territory. But the court ruled on March 6, 1857, that Scott was not free because Black people "had no rights which the white man was bound to respect; and the negro might justly and lawfully be reduced to slavery for his benefit."[253] That is to say, no persons of African descent had any standing under the U.S. Constitution.

Coming just three years after the passage of the Kansas-Nebraska Act, the Dred Scott decision is often regarded as the worst Supreme Court ruling of all time. Ironically, Judge McLean, who had presided over the Van Zandt case ten years earlier in the lower court, was now a justice of the U.S. Supreme Court. Perhaps Salmon Chase's arguments had finally gotten through to him because his was one of just two dissenting voices in the Dred Scott Decision.

There is no reason to believe Addison "Ad" White knew anything about Dred Scott or that it would have made any difference if he had. Late in 1856, White had shown up in Mechanicsburg, Ohio. A large, strong and generally imposing-looking individual, he was hired by Udney H. Hyde to work on his farm while Hyde was recovering from a broken ankle. It is thought that White had come from Flemingsville, Kentucky. Hyde likely knew or at least suspected he was a runaway slave, but he wasn't the only one.

White was anxious to have his wife, a free Black woman, join him. The two of them had been exchanging letters—understandable, but reckless under the circumstances. Allegations later "surfaced that Springfield Postmaster William K. Boggs had alerted federal authorities of White's whereabouts while handling letters from his wife."[254]

On May 21, 1857, White was inside Hyde's cabin when Deputy U.S. Marshals Benjamin P. Churchill and John C. Eliott (sometimes Elliott or Elliot) and a half dozen or so men from Kentucky passed by. Spotting them through the front window, White quickly sprang up the ladder to conceal himself in the loft, where he had stored a rifle, revolver, knife and axe.

While the Kentuckians were posted outside to ensure White didn't escape, the marshals forced their way into the cabin. Deputy Eliott saw a board move in the loft floor and fired a load of buckshot at it. He then scrambled up the ladder, poking his head through the opening. White immediately fired his rifle, but the ball was deflected by the barrel of Eliott's gun and tore through his ear. Falling to the floor below, Eliott screamed, "I am a dead man."[255]

An abolitionist and a true friend of the Black man, Hyde was a cagey individual. He purportedly helped as many as five hundred in their quest for freedom.[256] "Why didn't you go on up and get him? Damn you!" Hyde swore at the slave hunters.[257] He then whispered something to his daughter before loudly announcing, "Feed the chickens, Manda, they haven't been fed this morning."[258]

Manda started off to do as instructed. But when she was some distance from the cabin, she took off running. One of the marshals ordered her to stop or he would shoot, but she hollered back, "Shoot and be durned!"[259] She then continued running all the way to the "abolition hole" of Mechanicsburg. It wasn't long before a large group of armed citizens came running to White's assistance. The display of force dissuaded the posse from making any further efforts to capture him. Ordered to depart, the posse did so, leaving their quarry behind.

Six days later, the marshals returned to Mechanicsburg seeking White and Udney. (In some accounts, there is no break between the first and second appearance of the marshals.) Both were in hiding. In frustration, the marshals began rounding up those who had anything to do with defending the Black man. Russell Hyde (Udney's son), Charles Taylor, Edward Taylor and Hiram Gutride were arrested and bundled into a carriage. Before they could be hauled away, a local lawyer, William Pangborn, told them they wouldn't have to go if they just said the word.

The marshals appeared to be headed toward Urbana but turned south when they reached the crest of Clark's Hill. The entire neighborhood was now up in arms. David Rutan and Oliver Colwell overtook them on horseback but were driven back by threats and drawn revolvers. The rumor had spread that the prisoners were being taken back to Kentucky. As the excitement grew, even more men turned out.

The slave hunters were tracked through Catawba Station, Summerford and South Charleston, where they assaulted Clark County Sheriff John E. Layton. They beat him so severely that he suffered from his injuries for the rest of his life. They then continued on to Cedarville, where they were intercepted by the Greene County sheriff, "old man Lewis" (Daniel Lewis), who locked the marshals up in the Springfield jail.[260] Meanwhile, the prisoners were returned to Mechanicsburg.

Tried on June 9, Churchill and Eliott were released when Judge Humphrey H. Leavitt decided they had been acting within the scope of the Fugitive Slave Law of 1850—this despite the passage of Ohio's personal liberty laws less than two months before. He ruled that they had been "committed and confined for an act done in pursuance of the laws of the United States, and that they be, and are, wholly discharged from such commitment and confinement."[261]

The U.S. district attorney then sought to arrest and prosecute anyone who had been involved in harboring the fugitive. At this point, Salmon P. Chase, governor of Ohio, stepped in. He worked out a compromise. "The case was afterward settled by the citizens buying Addison for $800."[262] White and his wife, however, were never reunited, and he eventually remarried.

Chief Justice Taney was among those who believed that the institution of slavery benefited the slaves as well as their masters. As he once expressed in a letter, the slave's "life is usually cheerful and contented, and free from any distressing wants or anxieties. He is well taken care of in infancy, in sickness, and in old age."[263] People with his mindset couldn't understand why they persisted in running off. C.A. Withers was one of them.

Around 1850, Colonel Withers of Covington, Kentucky—superintendent of the Covington & Lexington Railroad—purchased Angela (aka Angeline) Broadus, an enslaved woman, from his nephew. The nephew was relocating to Missouri and apparently didn't want to separate the woman from her husband, Irvine (aka Irwin) Broadus, who was owned by a neighbor. Two years later, Irvine's owner died and his son decided to offer him for sale in the South. Once again, Withers stepped up to prevent the couple from being separated by purchasing the husband.

By all accounts, Withers was a "kindly master"—for a slave owner, anyway. "He located the pair in a good house, well and conveniently furnished, and treated them in the most kind manner," according to an article in the *Eaton Democrat.*[264] But over time, agents of the Underground Railroad began "tampering with the slaves"—a common complaint.[265] Finally, the couple made their escape on the evening of June 10, 1857.[266] After a few days, Withers learned that the runaways were being hidden in the lodging room of William M. Connolly, a reporter for the Cincinnati *Commercial.* The room was on the fifth floor of a building owned by Alphonso Taft in the heart of the city.

After watching the room all Friday evening, Deputy U.S. Marshals John C. Eliott and J.R. Anderson, along with two or three other men, raided it on Saturday, June 12. By Eliott's own admission, they were there hunting "niggers." He used a short ladder and smashed the transoms above the doors of various offices with a "single barrel pistol" in order to peek inside.[267] At the third door, Eliott struck the sash with his pistol, and it swung open. Through the doorway, he saw a table with a hat and plate of food sitting on it. The marshal knew he had found the fugitives, as he later testified, but before he could shoot or do anything, "the nigger stabbed me and pushed me back into the hall."[268] And a shot was fired—presumably by an unidentified Kentuckian who happened to be present.

Deputy Anderson immediately bashed in the door with a bed rail and saw both Irvine and Angela Broadus. "At this time the second shot was fired [presumably by the same Kentuckian], and the nigger fell."[269] Struck in the stomach, Irvine fell to the floor and was subdued by Anderson and his assistants after a short scuffle. Anderson then searched the suspect and found a knife, iron knuckles and a sword cane. Meanwhile, Eliott had retreated to the U.S. marshal's office in the customshouse across the street, where it was discovered he had been knifed twice, once in the left breast and once in the arm at the elbow.

Within thirty minutes, the Broaduses were taken to the courtroom for a hearing before Commissioner Edward R. Newhall. Convicted without benefit of counsel or witnesses, they were delivered to Colonel Withers in Covington just after noon. Having been gravely wounded, Irvine would live about six more weeks. Following his death, Angela was sold and resold. At the same time, Newhall issued a warrant for Connolly's arrest on the charge of violating the Fugitive Slave Act of 1850. When he heard he was a wanted man, the reporter fled to New York.

In February 1858, Deputy Marshal Eliott stopped in New York City while returning from Washington, D.C., and asked Marshal Rynders to assist him in arresting Connolly. Rynders designated one of his deputies, O'Keefe, to meet with Churchill at seven o'clock in the evening and then proceed to the newspaper where Connolly was employed. However, O'Keefe arrived early and sent for Connolly. He came down at once and was arrested.

Connolly's trial commenced on May 6, 1858. In his summarization to the jury, Corwin argued that they must be satisfied that his client knew the people he was sheltering were fugitive slaves. Apparently, they were. The jury found Connolly guilty as charged. It was the first case in which a person was convicted for simply harboring a fugitive slave. It was seen as a blow to states' rights because the laws of Kentucky were extended to Ohio. But Judge Humphrey Leavitt imposed a relatively light sentence—ten (or perhaps twenty) days in jail and a fine of ten dollars. The prisoner "was installed in the best room of the jail and furnished by the abolitionists of the city with bedstead and bedding and writing materials and with the best board that could be furnished."[270]

Each day visitors flocked to his jail cell, and it became fashionable for the ladies to bring him gifts of "fruit and other dainties." Public school teachers and church ministers called on him in organized bodies. Even educator Horace Mann paid a visit to Connolly while in town for the Unitarian Conference.

When it came time for Connolly's release, "the Turners [a German social club] and other societies of the city escorted him from jail with a torchlight procession headed by a band of music and a number of carriages, in which were seated Judge [John] Stallo and other prominent citizens."[271] Upon reaching Turner Hall, Connolly delivered a speech. He would go on to deliver many speeches in support of the Underground Railroad, donating any proceeds to the antislavery movement.

Beginning with the Kansas-Nebraska Act in 1854 and ending just before the outbreak of the Civil War in 1861, the Kansas Territory was a battleground. During that period, there was a series of violent confrontations between the antislavery "Free-Staters" and the pro-slavery "Border Ruffians," especially along the Kansas-Missouri border. The key issue was whether the Kansas Territory would enter the Union as a free state or a slave state. The Kansas-Nebraska Act, passed by a margin of one vote, had left the decision up to those who settled there.

Already a slave state, Missouri had a large population of Southerners and Southern sympathizers, many of whom sought to influence the voters of Kansas. In 1855, abolitionist John Brown arrived hoping to do likewise. Violence began to erupt later that same year. Then on the night of May 24, 1856, Brown, his sons and other zealots attacked the pro-slavery settlement of Pottawatomie Creek, dragged five pro-slavery men from their homes and slayed them with broadswords.

Three months later, Brown and his men took on some four hundred pro-slavery soldiers in the Battle of Osawatomie. As hostilities continued to rage over the course of several years, Horace Greeley's *New York Tribune* branded the territory "Bleeding Kansas." After Brown departed Kansas, newly appointed territorial governor John W. Geary took office. In time, he was able to negotiate an intermittent peace. Finally, the questioned was settled when Kansas entered the Union as a free state in 1858. The next year, the violence came to an end.

"Border Ruffians" were basically terrorists who threated to kill anyone who opposed slavery. *Library of Congress.*

John Brown's reputation was diminished by his murder of five pro-slavers at the Pottawatomie, Kansas. *Library of Congress.*

Following closely on the lead of Ohio and Wisconsin, Vermont passed a personal liberty law in 1858. However, it then took it one step farther, declaring that no one would be denied citizenship due to African descent. But, at the same time, Arkansas enacted a law that called for the enslavement of any free Black people who remained within the state. The gap was widening between the free and slave states.

While prowling around the abolitionist stronghold of Oberlin in search of some runaways belonging to his uncle's estate, Anderson D. Jennings learned of another fugitive he wasn't looking for. According to historian William Cochran, "Jennings arrived in Oberlin late in August, 1858, and went to Wack's hotel, which he made the base for operations."[272] He was a professional slave catcher from Maysville, Kentucky, and Chauncey Wack—"an openly racist, anti-abolitionist Democrat"—was happy to welcome him.[273]

Jennings was soon joined by two men—U.S. Deputy Marshal A.P. Dayton and another named Warren. They told him that a Black man answering to the description of John Price—commonly known as "Nigger John"—was living in the area. He had fled from his master, John G. Bacon of Mason County, Kentucky. Coincidentally, Bacon was a friend of the slave catcher.

Recognizing an opportunity when he saw one, Jennings contacted Bacon to authorize Price's arrest. Richard P. Mitchell, another professional slave catcher, delivered a power of attorney to him. He then went to Columbus to obtain the assistance of U.S. Deputy Marshal Jacob K. Lowe. Together, they went to U.S. Commissioner Sterne Chittenden to obtain a warrant for the arrest of "John, a fugitive and person escaped from service by him owed to John G. Bacon."[274]

On Friday night, September 10, Jennings, Mitchell, Lowe and Samuel Davis—the last an acting deputy sheriff of Franklin County—had a conference with Dayton and Warren at the hotel. "Both Dayton and Warren said that it would be dangerous to attempt to arrest John Price in Oberlin; that some scheme must be contrived for getting him out of town so that he could be seized and carried off without raising a disturbance."[275]

And Warren suggested Lewis D. Boynton was a man who could be trusted to help them.

At a Democratic party meeting in Lorain the previous year, Boynton had put forth the following resolution: "*Resolved*, That 'Negro Equality,' 'Bleeding Kansas,' 'Horace Greely [*sic*],' and the [Salmon P.] Chase administration are the four greatest political humbugs of the age, and that it is the duty of the democrats to see to it that at the coming election, this mongrel combination is routed, *horse, foot, and dragoon.*"[276]

On Saturday, September 11, 1858, two slave hunters arrived at General Boynton's house, just outside Oberlin.[277] They remained for two days. On Monday morning, Boynton's twelve-year-old son, Shakespeare, drove his father's buggy to Oberlin. He located the Black man known as John or "Little John" and told him his father wanted to hire him to dig potatoes. While he wasn't interested in doing the work himself, John Price agreed to help the boy recruit someone else who would. However, when they had gone about half a mile, another carriage drove up behind them. Price found himself "seized from behind by the arms, dragged from the buggy, pinioned, and placed in the carriage between his *brave* Kentucky captors"— Lowe, Mitchell and Davis.[278]

While Shakespeare continued on to Wack's Hotel to report back to Jennings, "the slave was driven over to Wellington, eight miles away, where he was made a prisoner at the Wadsworth hotel, it being intended to take him south by the first train and introduce him to slavery."[279] They were soon joined by Jennings.

Fortunately for Price, he was recognized by an Oberlin student who raised the alarm. As word of his kidnapping spread throughout Oberlin, a crowd estimated at six hundred marched in a silent procession to Wellington. Coincidentally, another sizeable crowd had already gathered there, drawn by a large fire.

"People came in from Grafton, La Grange, Rochester and New London, on the railroad, and from the surrounding country in buggies to see the fire, and when the fire was out, joined the crowd around the hotel, hoping to see something exciting."[280] When word reached them of the kidnapping, they surrounded the hotel and were joined by reinforcements from Oberlin. They attempted to negotiate Price's release with Marshal Jacob, but to no avail.

Spotting Price looking out a window in the attic, the rescuers obtained a ladder. They then "began climbing to the second story porch, they backed up to the attic, and retired to a room which had a small fan-shaped window and one door with a rope fastening."[281] Although Jennings and

Mitchell were large men, and all four of them were heavily armed, the mob managed to help Price escape and then rushed him back to Oberlin. In the end, "No one was hurt, not a shilling's damage was done, not a shot fired, and the boy saved."[282]

Upon reaching Oberlin, Price was hidden in the home of future college president James. H. Fairchild. According to historian William Cochran, "Professor Fairchild's attic was chosen, much against his will, because he was about the last man in town who would be suspected of violating any law, no matter how bad the law might be."[283] The following day, Price was sent on his way to Canada. However, he reportedly died not long afterward.

This bold violation of the Fugitive Slave Act rankled the federal government. A federal grand jury in Cleveland was convened and quickly moved to indict thirty-seven people—nine of them African Americans—for their involvement in the slave's rescue. Oddly, they were all Republicans, although many Democrats were said to have participated in the rescue as well and boasted of their involvement, a fact that was pointed out by several Cleveland newspapers. Incredibly, Lewis Boynton served as one of the jurors.

Among those indicted were Simeon Bushnell, a store clerk who had driven John to Canada and, ostensibly, the group's leader; Reverend Henry Peck, a faculty member at Oberlin College; Reverend James M. Fitch, a

A monument to the Oberlin-Wellington Rescuers was erected in Oberlin. *Authors' collection.*

missionary; and Charles Henry Langston, older brother of John Mercer Langston. Although Bushnell had started late for Wellington "because he wanted 'a good rig and a man with a gun,' [he still] passed nearly everybody on the road."[284] Another Black man, John Copeland Jr., was also indicted. He had escorted Price to Canada.[285]

Some of the defendants posted bond, but others remained in jail under protest until the trial was scheduled to begin on April 5, 1859. Their counsel—Franklin T. Backus, Rufus P. Spalding, Albert G. Riddle and Seneca O. Griswold—also engaged in some astute legal wrangling, forcing the court to try each of the defendants individually and with a new jury. This served to keep the issue alive far longer than it might have been otherwise. Unfortunately, they could muster only a weak defense based on principle.

After Bushnell was convicted, the same jury—all Democrats—heard Langston's case, despite protests that they could not be impartial. He was convicted as well. Then Langston, a prominent African American leader in the community, defiantly addressed the court:

> *I say, that if ever again a man is seized near me, and is about to be carried Southward as a slave, before any legal investigation has been had, I shall hold it to be my duty, as I held it that day, to secure for him, if possible, a legal inquiry into the character of the claim by which he is held. And I go farther; I say that if it is adjudged illegal to procure even such an investigation, then we are thrown back upon those last defenses of our rights, which cannot be taken from us, and which God gave us that we need not be slaves.*[286]

Showing leniency, Judge Bliss fined Bushnell $1,000 and sentenced him to sixty days in jail and Langston $100 and twenty days. The thirteen residents of Wellington, considered accomplices, were each fined $20 and costs and confined in jail for twenty-four hours. "Twelve of the Oberlin men remained in jail at Cleveland, but all the prisoners had a rather enjoyable time," according to historian William Neff.[287]

It was eventually agreed that the United States would drop charges against all of the rescuers provided that the State of Ohio abandoned suits against Lowe, Jennings and the other kidnappers. When the rescuers returned to Oberlin, they were accorded a hero's welcome. Langston then joined with others to found the Ohio Anti-Slavery Society.

However, Deputy Lowe then sued Professors Fairchild and Peck, as well as Judge Carpenter, in the Superior Court at Columbus for $20,000. He charged that they had conspired to have him imprisoned. After two and a half years, the charges were dismissed at the plaintiff's cost, meaning Lowe had to pay the cost of the suit. One newspaper described him as "probably about an average specimen of the United States Marshals under the old regime."[288]

# 10

# THE PARSON HAS TURNED

*The parson has turned; for, on charge of his own,*
*Who goeth a warfare, or hunting, alone?*
—John Greenleaf Whittier, "The Hunters of Men"

Proponents of slavery often justified it by claiming that the enslaved were ill-prepared to survive on their own. They conveniently overlooked the fact that those held in bondage had been trained by their masters since infancy to be subservient and dependent. Or that they were often denied educational opportunities in an effort to keep them in ignorance. And that independent thinking might be punished. Nor did they explain how some free Black people were actually more prosperous than their white neighbors, despite having fewer civil liberties.

When there was a fugitive slave case that appeared to support this viewpoint, pro-slavery newspapers could be counted on to play it up. Such was the case when Mason Barbour, a runaway slave, was arrested on March 25, 1859, about eight to ten miles outside Columbus.

Barbour, who was said to be forty-five, had escaped on or about July 20, 1856. During his nearly three years of freedom, he had been living in the Columbus area and often preached in the Methodist church. But after he was captured by U.S. Deputy Marshal Jacob K. Lowe, he "appeared perfectly willing to return to slavery, as he said he had found freedom arduous to support. He had worked hard, he said, and had not a half-dime to show for his labor."[289]

Taken before U.S. Commissioner Charles C. Brown in Cincinnati, Barbour admitted he was a slave and owed service to Absalom Ridgely. When the ruling was made, he purportedly exclaimed, "God bless you, massa…I'se satisfied I rise to no 'stinction in dis country. I'se swin back wid ye to yer ole home."[290] It was likely his fear of punishment talking, and it is also possible his dialect was exaggerated by the writer for effect.

On April 6, Ridgely took possession of Barbour and returned with him upriver to his home, some twenty miles from Wheeling, [West] Virginia. Before departing, he said, "Mason is a valuable and reliable negro, and this his running away caused great surprise, as the boy had always seemed satisfied with his condition."[291] As was often the case, Ridgely preferred to think that Barbour's obsequious behavior was born out of his esteem for his master rather than the absolute power he exercised over his life.

The Fugitive Slave Act of 1850 was designed to process cases as efficiently as possible. As an added incentive, the U.S. commissioners were paid five dollars for every person of color they freed and ten dollars for everyone they remanded back to his owner. The rationale for this implicit bias in the law was that the commissioner had to do more—in essence, arrange for the fugitive to be returned to the slaveholder. Most of the time, however, the owner or his agent took immediate custody and already had a hack waiting outside. What could be quicker?

That was what happened to Lewis Early. An enslaved man owned by George Killgore of Cabell County, [West] Virginia, Early was taken to Ohio in 1856. He settled in Ross County, where he worked part time for J. Robinson, a relative of his owner.

Several years later, Kilgore gave his son, James, who lived in Kentucky, power of attorney, authorizing him to pursue and retrieve Early. After obtaining a warrant from Commissioner Charles C. Brown of Cincinnati, James traveled to Ross County to arrest Early. He was accompanied by Deputy U.S. Marshal William L. Manson and a friend named Thompson. Because he felt Early might recognize him, James dyed his hair and whiskers.

On March 25, 1859, the three men surprised Early as he was chopping wood with another Black man. Manson immediately trained a revolver on Early and ordered him to surrender. He did. As the fugitive was being handcuffed, his companion jumped on a horse and rode off to alert people at a nearby farm that Early was being abducted.

According to an article in *The Liberator*, the slave hunters began walking toward the nearest railroad station, traveling "some fifteen or twenty miles

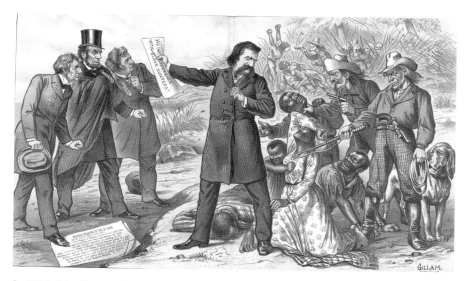

In 1853, John Logan of Illinois sponsored a law banning African Americans from settling in his state. *Library of Congress.*

through mud and mire."[292] Upon reaching Buckskin Township, "they were met by a constable and a large posse of men, armed with a warrant issued by Robert Coyner, Justice of the Peace," charging the three of them with kidnapping.[293]

Outnumbered, the men offered no resistance and were transported directly to Coyner's office. In front of several hundred assembled citizens, Justice Coyner demanded to know by what authority they had arrested Early. When presented with the warrant from the commissioner, Coyner recognized that it was legitimate and told the crowd he was bound to obey it. He dropped the kidnapping charges and released the slave catchers.

Anxious to be on their way, Manson, Kilgore and Thompson escorted Early to the Lyndon station of the Cincinnati and Marietta Railroad. The *Buffalo Daily Courier* noted, "A great crowd had gathered and [the men] were compelled to draw their revolvers to prevent a rescue."[294] Finally, they mounted the train to Cincinnati.

Early was represented by John Jolliffe, J.W. Caldwell and Thomas Powell in a hearing before Commissioner Brown. According to testimony by Robinson and others, Early had originally been brought to the home of Robinson in Ross County by a man named Schetzer. He had with him an emancipation paper signed by Kilgore, who was Robinson's brother-in-law, and three witnesses.

Although the weight of testimony suggested that Early was a free man, he could not prove it. Witnesses testified that his deed of emancipation had been lost in a fire in October of the same year. While Ohio law did not require a free Black man to have such proof, it was silent on what to do if he could not produce it.

Kilgore's argument was pretty much that his father was a lunatic who had since been placed under guardianship. Period. Yet Brown ruled in Killgore's favor and, as the *Cleveland Daily Leader* noted, thereby collected a larger fee. Early was placed in a hack and rushed across the Ohio River to Covington, Kentucky, before a writ of habeas corpus signed by Judge Humphrey Leavitt could be served. So Jolliffe immediately brought a $2,000 damage suit against Killgore for false imprisonment. In the end, the slave owner offered to sell Lewis Early to the abolitionists for $1,150 but settled for $425.

Enforcing the Fugitive Slave Act placed federal marshals in a difficult position. While some had no compunctions about upholding the law, others found themselves on the horns of a moral dilemma. And a few became the target of their neighbors' righteous indignation. U.S. Deputy Marshal Ezekiel T. Cox was one.

"The emboldened men-stealers have again polluted the soil of Ohio, and borne off another victim"—so wrote the *Holmes County Republican* when Charley (some sources say William) Jackson was taken into custody in Zanesville by Deputy Cox.

For three years, Jackson had lived in Belmont County. Then on May 2, 1859, a "miscreant" named Honeycutt, assisted by an unnamed Black man, decoyed Jackson to Zanesville where Deputy Cox was waiting. After placing the prisoner in irons, Cox carted him off for a hearing before U.S. Commissioner James Cochran.

The case was heard in secret, behind the locked door of the commissioner's office. The slave catchers represented that the Black man was the property of Colonel James M. Jackson. Commissioner Cochran deemed him a fugitive from labor and remanded back to slavery in Clarksburg, [West] Virginia.

But while Jackson was in jail, a writ of habeas corpus was procured and served on the sheriff. This case was heard before Judge Lucious P. Marsh. To the surprise of many, the judge ordered him released on the grounds that he was held illegally. It was reported that "no sooner were these words out of the mouth of the Judge, than Mr. Cox, whose posse surrounded the negro, pounced upon him, declaring him his prisoner, &c., and calling on everybody present to aid him in keeping possession of him, &c."[295]

Some who escaped from slavery then returned in an attempt to free their families. *Authors' collection.*

In direct defiance of Judge Marsh, Cox rushed the Black man out the back door of the courthouse to Fourth Street and into a waiting hack. The hack then made a mad dash to the depot in order to catch the train that was due to be arriving from Wheeling. Cox had arranged for a special force of armed deputies with revolvers cocked to guard them.

As reported in the *New York Tribune*:

> *A large number of blacks had preceded the carriage to the depot, and on its arrival there, an assault was made, with a view of rescuing the prisoner. Many of the assailants fought bravely, but they were speedily dispersed—the bystanders, without reference to political preferences, voluntarily aiding the officers in maintaining possession of the fugitive.*[296]

Designed to serve as the state capital, Stone Academy was the center of abolitionist activity in Zanesville. *Photo by Ford Walker.*

The *Detroit Free Press* provided a detailed account of the melee "between the white and colored population in which the use of pistols, bricks, stones, canes, chairs, fists, boards, car-coupling pins, and jack-knives played a more or less active part."[297] Although many were bruised and bloodied, no one was known to have died. On the other hand, the *Freemont Weekly Journal* claimed, "A large crowd assembled at the depot, but no attempt was made to rescue."[298]

Once the crowd had dispersed, Marshal Cox was served with another writ of habeas corpus, but to no avail. As the *Courier* put it, "The fugitive was held by the Marshal and his posse until the next morning, when he was placed on board a train and conveyed back to slavery, thus saving the Union!"[299] The marshal, however, did not emerge unscathed.

The father of Ohio representative Samuel S. "Sunset" Cox, Ezekiel Cox had been a member of the Market Street Baptist Church of Zanesville for twenty years. But when he arrested Charley Jackson on a warrant in his capacity as deputy marshal, the church resolved that he "had participated in the fugitive slave case in a manner wholly unwarranted by the word of God, and by so doing had aggrieved his brethren in the church, and brought dishonor on the cause of Christ and the Church of which he is a member."[300] Therefore, he was expelled from the congregation.

The *Brooklyn Daily Eagle* described Cox as the victim of a modern inquisition. In his defense, it asserted that the fugitive, Charley Jackson, "ran away from a kind and humane master, stole a horse, saddle, and bridle, and committed a criminal offense besides of the most atrocious character, upon a poor, weak white girl."[301]

Later in May, Reuben Johnson, a Black man, was arrested by a marshal on the charge of attempting to rescue Jackson. The *State Journal* observed, "The Marshal is like the monkey in the litigation of the cats about the division of the cheese, in the fable; justice may be satisfied, but the Marshal is not."[302]

All runaway slaves who elected to stay in Ohio hoped to avoid attention. Some felt they would be safer in big cities, others in small towns. John Tyler (some sources say John Rice) was a thirty-three-year-old "mulatto" who lived in Mount Gilead with his wife and child and had done so for nearly eight years. However, he was suspected of being a fugitive slave, and U.S. Deputy Marshal William Manson was authorized to arrest him. On September 15,

Slave patrols or "paddy rollers" scoured the Border States, looking for fugitives from slavery. *Authors' collection.*

1859, the marshal learned that Tyler had been living at Oberlin and Mount Gilead under the name of Tobe Price.

A month later, a man who identified himself as D.C. Watson hired Tyler and his friend, Henry Alfred, also a man of color, to work in a saloon he was planning to open in Columbus. Although they knew nothing about their employer, they agreed to go with him. The two friends traveled as far as Delaware, where they stayed with some of Tyler's relatives while Watson continued on to Columbus.

The following morning, October 28, 1859, Watson met them in Columbus with a party of men. Tyler was seized at the railroad depot by Deputy Marshal Jacob Lowe and Constable Robert Mitchell, along with several others, including Deputy Manson.

"A general fight was the result, some for and some against the fugitive's arrest," according to the *Cincinnati Enquirer*. "The established rules for fisticuffs were disregarded here, for they took it rough-and-tumble, under wagons, drays and horses."[303]

Despite being outnumbered, Tyler, who was six feet tall and weighed 190 pounds, fought them off for at least half an hour, even as Lowe repeatedly hit him on the head with a heavy cane. Manson said the Black man "hurled him about as if he had been a boy, and several others realized the strength of his muscles, and the sharpness of his teeth, in a very unpleasant degree."[304] The lawman's right had was "scarified," and a man named Mitchell had the skin stripped from one of his thumbs.

Alfred was also roughed up when he tried to intervene, as were several other bystanders who attempted to rescue Tyler from Manson's posse. The officers did not show a warrant or any other documentation to justify their actions. However, they told some fifty to seventy witnesses that Tyler had been committing a robbery. Not all believed it.

After Manson and his men forced the fugitive onto the 8:40 a.m. train bound for Cincinnati, they departed. But Tyler's supporters did not give up hope. According to a newspaper account, "A telegraphic dispatch was sent to Xenia, notifying persons there to procure a writ of *habeas corpus* for the fugitive."[305]

Judge William White quickly issued the writ.[306] He then ordered Greene County Sheriff Samuel Krumbaugh to take custody of Tyler and present him to the Common Pleas Court along with those who had detained him. When the train arrived around noon, Krumbaugh promptly boarded it. He "found that the negro was locked up in the closet in the front car, and guarded by some person [*sic*] who it was afterward found were U.S. Deputy

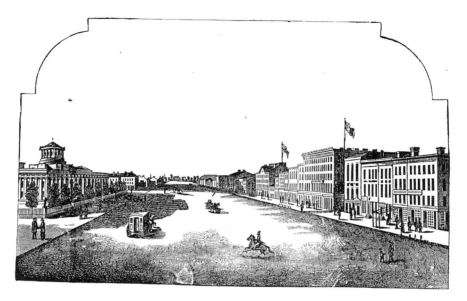

Several Underground Railroad routes passed through or near Columbus. *Authors' collection.*

Marshal, W.L. Manson and his assistants."[307] Although he successfully served the writ on Manson, the deputy did not obey it.

An estimated 150 African Americans had also assembled at the Xenia depot and swarmed onto the train, determined to release the prisoner at all costs. Manson prepared to resist them, but the would-be rescuers fled as soon as the conductor gave the signal for the train to depart. Because he had no jurisdiction outside of Greene County, Sheriff Krumbaugh wired ahead to Sheriff Henry Kessler of Hamilton County to meet him at the depot so he could serve the writ.

It so happened that attorney James Elliott of Xenia was on board the train. Volunteering to serve as counsel for the prisoner, he asked Manson to let him see the legal paperwork, as well as his client. Manson denied both requests, saying that he would have opportunity to do so when they reached Cincinnati and placed Tyler on trial.

As the train pulled into Cincinnati, there was a large group of men at the depot waiting to assist Manson and his party, including H.H. Robinson and several officers of the Independent Detective Police. However, Sheriff Kessler and his deputies were nowhere to be found.

A frightened-looking Tyler was hauled out of the closet in manacles and bundled off the train into an awaiting hack. The vehicle barreled through the back streets of the city until it reached the customhouse. It was followed closely by another hack carrying James Elliott, who was concerned that he might be given a hearing without counsel.

The helpless prisoner was rushed up the stairs to the marshal's office. Several men greeted him and shook his hand, but when asked if he knew them, he shook his head. He was then ushered into Commissioner Edward Newhall's office. Only at this point did Elliott have the opportunity to speak to his client and inform him he would handle his defense.

In the briefest of exchanges, Tyler told Elliott that he was a free man and could prove it. He said his wife had property in Mount Gilead and would pay him if he took his case. But before Elliott even had a chance to examine the writ, Newhall started the proceeding with George E. Pugh seated as the attorney for the prisoner.

Elliott interjected that he was Tyler's counsel and asked for a postponement so that witnesses could be brought from Morrow County. But in an *Alice in Wonderland* moment, "The Court replied that they would examine the witnesses present first, and consider that question afterward."[308]

Henry P. Samuels, an attorney from Barbersville, Cabell County, Virginia, testified that he had known Tyler for many years as a slave of Samuel (or, possibly, Solomon) Thornburg, who had passed away in December 1854. At about the same time, the enslaved man had fled the state.

Although Elliott expressed his desire to cross-examine Samuels, Newhall would not allow him to do so. Elliott then argued that the right had never been denied in any court, but Newhall still refused, saying he did not want to be interrupted.

James L. Thornburg, son of Samuel, also testified that he knew Tyler as his father's slave and that the name recorded in their family Bible was "Tobe" or "John Tyler." He stated that the prisoner now belonged to his sister, Elizabeth Griffin. He fixed the date of Tyler's escape as the last day of February 1854. Once again, Elliott asked for the right to cross-examine the witness but was denied.

Newhall then removed some papers from his pocket, identifying them as depositions. He said that together with the testimony he had heard, they established the facts of the case. He then ordered the marshal to deliver the prisoner to the claimant.

"Mr. Elliot [*sic*] here interrupted," it was reported, "and asked if this man was to be hurried into slavery without an opportunity to cross-examine his accusers or to offer testimony that had been presented."[309] He declared that "the most wretched murderer, would not be condemned without

138

a hearing and without an opportunity to make a defence."[310] However, Newhall ruled that the case was at an end. He then remanded Tyler into the custody of attorney Thornburg. The entire hearing had occupied no more than fifteen minutes.

Tyler was hurried out of the building across the Ohio River, where he was placed in the Covington, Kentucky jail. Along the way, he purportedly shook hands with Thornburg.

While many Americans were troubled by country's continued tolerance of slavery within its borders, few were willing to take up arms against it. John Brown was the exception. He had already done so in Kansas and would do so again. An ardent—some would say fanatical—abolitionist, Brown had spent his formative years in Ohio and had been active in the Underground Railroad. But it wasn't enough. He believed it was time for a "forcible separation of the connection between master and slave."[311]

On the night of October 15, 1859, Brown led thirteen other white men and five Black in an assault on the United States arsenal at Harpers Ferry, [West] Virginia. With the rifles and other weapons he expected to capture, Brown may have hoped to lead a slave rebellion, although he would deny it. For three days, Brown and his men held the armory against eighty-eight U.S. Marines, all the while expecting that two to five hundred slaves would rally to his cause.

In the end, Brown was taken alive, ten of his followers were killed and seven others were captured when the armory was retaken by the Marines commanded by Brevet Colonel Robert E. Lee. Tried and hanged for treason, Brown was transformed into a martyr whose death may have been the spark that lit the fuse of the powder keg that exploded into the Civil War. One of those who witnessed the hanging was John Wilkes Booth—the actor who would assassinate President Abraham Lincoln five years later.

## 11

# THE HOME OF THE WHITE

*What right have they here in the home of the white,*
*Shadowed o'er by our banner of Freedom and Right?*
*—John Greenleaf Whittier, "The Hunters of Men"*

The Fugitive Slave Act was, in effect, a license to steal. On any given day or night, people of color—and, occasionally, others—were simply stolen from the free state of Ohio. Judicial oversight was inconsistent. Black Ohioans had few rights. And the system was rife with corruption as the case of James "Charles" Waggoner illustrates. Early in October 1859, Waggoner, an African American man living in Cincinnati, went missing. For several months, his friends and family did not realize he was gone. But by then it was too late—or nearly so.

Waggoner was unemployed. So when two men—William Stewart and Michael Weaver—approached him with the prospect of a job in Fulton, a Cincinnati suburb, he did not hesitate to go with them. Stewart was no stranger. Waggoner had known him many years before in Georgetown. After they shook hands, his old friend "promised to give him work, stating that he had some bowlders [*sic*] he wished to have sorted."[312]

Upon arriving at their destination, however, the men jumped the Black man. Placing a pistol to his head, they forced him into a boat and rowed across the Ohio River to Jamestown, Kentucky, just above Newport. According to the *Cincinnati Press*, Stewart and Weaver were acting "under pretense that he was the slave of some person in Virginia, which they had been employed to pursue and recover."[313] That was likely a lie. After they reached the opposite shore, they took their prisoner to Weaver's house and confined him in a cellar that contained a bed.

By chance, a Newport police officer named Stone had been spying on the house, hoping to catch a band of counterfeiters. When he heard that three persons had shown up there, he rushed in with a posse and discovered Waggoner. Because Stewart and Weaver told them the Black man was a fugitive slave, Stone dutifully escorted him to the Newport jail for safekeeping. But the slave catchers made no further claim to him, probably because they had none.

Through a tip from Jonathan Horsfall, the Newport jail keeper, Stewart and Weaver were arrested in Cincinnati on October 19, 1859, and charged with kidnapping a "free Negro." Following an examination before Judge David P. Lowe of the Police Court, they were confined in jail to await the next grand jury session. But in the aftermath of the sacking of the *Free South*—Kentucky's only antislavery newspaper—and the dumping of its type and presses in the Ohio River, the atmosphere in Newport was so highly charged that no witnesses dared cross the river to testify. Consequently, the kidnappers were set free after the grand jury failed to find a true bill against them.

Waggoner, nevertheless, remained in jail. By the draconian laws of Kentucky, it was incumbent upon him to prove he was a free man. If he could not do so, he was assumed to be guilty. Mayor Edmund Hawkins of Newport sentenced Waggoner to six months in jail while advertising him in the newspapers as a fugitive slave. Meanwhile, Stewart and Weaver bided their time in hope of obtaining a seventy-five-dollar reward should the prisoner go to auction.

At the end of six months, Waggoner remained unclaimed, likely because no one could prove ownership. Although his parents had visited him from Bantam, Clermont County, Ohio, their word counted for nothing. Only the testimony of a white citizen could save him—that and $200 to $300 for "jail fees."[314]

Having pronounced Waggoner a fugitive slave, Mayor Hawkins moved forward with plans to auction him off in June 1860—"thus transforming, by process said to be strictly in conformity with the laws of the locality, a free inhabitant of Ohio into a slave in Kentucky in a little over half a year."[315] He was placed in a buggy and driven to the slave market in Alexandria.

As reported in the *Pomeroy Weekly Telegraph*,

> *An injunction, however, which had been sued out, was immediately dispatched, but the party having the negro in charge, were a few minutes*

*ahead. As the party neared Alexandria, Col. Smalley, with one of his fastest horses, drove up, passed the pursuers and reached the Sheriff's party, informed them of the injunction on the way, took the negro into his buggy and reached Alexandria first.*[316]

Surprisingly, Waggoner's plight had not attracted the attention of Ohio Republicans who would certainly have made political capital of it. But the *Cincinnati Daily Press* began to stir things up when it asked the citizens of Cincinnati to contribute money to save Waggoner from the auction block.

Finally, Waggoner's luck changed. Attorney George P. Webster of Newport learned of his situation. A native of Connecticut, Webster had settled in Kentucky after spending three years in the gold fields of California. He became convinced that Waggoner had been treated unfairly. At least twice, Webster filed a writ of habeas corpus, only to have it shot down on the grounds that Kentucky law presumed the prisoner to be a slave unless he could prove otherwise.

Then, on June 4, 1860, Webster finagled a hearing before Mayor Hawkins when neither a county nor a circuit judge was available. John Whiteman, Eliza S. Whiteman and Mary Miller all testified that they had known James Waggoner and his father, Peter, since 1852. During that time, the Waggoners had resided in Ohio as free men and there was never any suspicion that they might be otherwise.

In an affidavit, Joseph Thomas, a resident of Cincinnati, stated that he had employed Waggoner for about a year and that his father, Peter, had come to see him during that time. Peter's own affidavit claimed that he had been freed in 1828 by the will of his master—also named Peter Waggoner—who had resided in Wythe County, Virginia. He had then moved to Ohio in 1831. James was subsequently born in Brown County and had never been in Virginia. However, Peter's affidavit was disregarded because of his race.

An unnamed witness from Virginia asserted that Peter Waggoner had, indeed, been set free by his master, but that the will had been annulled in 1843. Another claimed the defendant matched the description of an enslaved man who had run away from Jacob Waggoner five years earlier but admitted he had never personally seen him. And yet another testified that Jacob Waggoner was too poor to own a slave. All the while, James Waggoner's freedom hung in the balance.

A statement was read from Jacob Waggoner in which he stated he had lost a "negro" a year before, including a "very luminous description of

England's Society for the Abolition of Slavery adopted this seal in the 1780s. *Library of Congress.*

him, which," the *Cincinnati Daily Press* observed, "like political platforms and phrenological delineations…admits of a very wide latitude of construction: 'He is tal slime made and has a grate kwantity of wite in his ize, and a downcast luk [*sic*].'"[317]

After hearing the testimony, Hawkins decided Waggoner was, in fact, a fugitive slave. He was immediately taken by the jailer, Jonathan Horsfall; the postmaster, Dr. J.Q.A. Foster; and one or two others in a carriage to Alexandria, the county seat, to be sold. They moved quickly so that attorney Webster would be unable to obtain and serve an injunction to stop the sale. Not long after they departed, Colonel Smalley set out after them on his fastest horse. When he overtook them, he gave his horse to Sheriff H.D. Helm, who had ridden out to meet them so he could hurry back to Alexandria and make all necessary preparations.

Although Webster reached Alexandria just three minutes after Waggoner, he found that the Black man had already been sold in secret to Dr. Foster, the local postmaster, for $700. Afterward, the prisoner was transported to Lexington and placed for sale in the "negro-pens of that city," while Webster returned to Newport.[318] When word got out about Waggoner's mistreatment, the city was in such an uproar that Foster began to reconsider his options.

In a letter dated June 6, 1860, he acknowledged he was present with a number of other men at the sale of Waggoner at Alexandria on the previous Monday and purchased him because he believed he was enslaved per the ruling of Mayor Hawkins. "He has not yet been sold by me, however," Foster wrote, "and I now propose, if the facts can be established of his being a free boy, to the satisfaction of any Court in Kentucky, I will cheerfully give him his freedom; or further, in event of his having been a slave, I will sell him to his sympathizers for the amount I paid for him."[319]

No doubt, Webster's dogged pursuit of justice for Waggoner was having an effect. As the *Cincinnati Daily Press* had previously noted, "The Messrs. Webster have no motive in the matter but to see that justice is done....They have not been retained by anyone but the negro, who is unable to pay them anything. They have spent money in his behalf, however, believing him to be free, and will do so again. One of them signed the bond to stay the sale."[320]

At the risk of his own freedom, Waggoner's father traveled to Newport, but any evidence he had was rejected out of hand, as was his previous affidavit. Another notice from Foster was posted in the *Cincinnati Commercial* of July 30, 1860, in which he attested to the events leading up to the kidnapping of Waggoner. According to Foster, two years earlier Sheriff Helm had formed a secret organization composed of several influential Democrats from each precinct. Their intent was to pack the various conventions throughout the county to ensure that only people of their choosing would be nominated for public office.

Foster went on to explain that when he had "purchased the colored boy known as Charles (aka James) Waggoner" who was sold by Sheriff Helm the previous month, he had been in league with the sheriff and that they were to share equally in the profits. Helm replied that Foster was an "almost demented inebriate" and "not responsible for his statement."[321]

Through Webster's perseverance, Waggoner came up for trial on August 15, 1860, before Judge Moore of the Campbell County Circuit Court. Foster claimed he was half owner of Waggoner with Sheriff Helm. He asked that the bond he had posted for the purchase money should be canceled should Waggoner go free. Helm denied any interest in Waggoner and claimed he sold him in accordance with the law. Neither man offered any testimony which would prove Waggoner was enslaved. But Waggoner had a number of witnesses in his defense.

Nancy Spiers of Brown County said she was present at the house of Peter and Rachel Waggoner when James was born in 1840 and knew him for two and a half years. David Osborne, a resident of Bethel, Clermont County, said that the Waggoners came to live on his farm in April 1849 when James was about nine or ten years old. They remained there for nearly three years. The man being held in the Newport jail he recognized as James, their son. The Waggoners were regarded as free persons of color. The depositions of Levi Dunham and others stated the same.

John Whiteman testified that he knew Peter and Rachel and James in 1855–56 when they were on his brother, James F. Whiteman's, farm in Clark County and that James was the same person he saw in the Newport jail. As a result of their testimony, the Kentucky court declared James Waggoner a free man.

Two months after Waggoner was originally sold at an auction, Judge Moore granted him his freedom on August 16, 1860. The courtroom was nearly filled to capacity when Moore handed down his decision:

> From the proof in this case there can be no doubt but the plaintiff is a free man; wherefore it is adjudged that the injunction herein be perpetuated, and that the sale of plaintiff be taken for nought; that he be released from custody and enjoy the freedom in some other country than this Commonwealth. And as defendants are officers, and plaintiff is in their custody by force of law, there can be no judgment against them for costs.[322]

Now that Waggoner was a free man, the *Cincinnati Daily Press* described him as "of feeble intellect, but looks like a stubborn customer to manage, and throughout his protracted imprisonment, and vicissitudes and excitements, has exhibited much endurance."[323] He returned to Cincinnati with George Webster, where he was met by his friends.

Once again, a warrant was issued against Stewart and Weaver and they found themselves facing Judge Lowe on the very same charges—kidnapping a free Black man. And once again, Waggoner related the story about how he was kidnapped by his old friend, Stewart, and his companion, Weaver. He was forced to repeat his story several times by Colonel Sullivan, counsel for the defense, who sought to trip him up. Another witness testified he heard

Weaver say that he had taken a "Negro" to Kentucky, for which he would receive $50 and an additional $500 from the slave's master.

So strong was the case against the two men that it was expected that the next grand jury would send it on to the criminal court. However, when Waggoner failed to show for the grand jury hearing in September, the prosecuting attorney recommended that charges against Weaver and Stewart be dropped. But it wasn't Waggoner's fault. He had been kidnapped and sold into slavery once more and, as far as can be determined, was never seen again.

Although a Democrat and a member of the state legislature—his vote had kept Kentucky from seceding from the Union—George Webster had risked the wrath of the local community. He would subsequently resign his office at the outbreak of the Civil War, move north and receive a commission as a captain in the Union army, rising to the rank of colonel.[324] He later became a prominent member of New York's infamous Tamany Hall—although he kept his reputation for honesty.

Sometime during the latter part of May 1860, three enslaved brothers escaped from their owners near Germantown, Kentucky. After making some inquiries, Reed and Pollock, the slaveholders, learned that the fugitives had settled just outside the town of Iberia in Morrow County, Ohio. Iberia was home to Iberia College, founded by abolitionist Reverend George Gordon. The school was open to both men and women of all races. Therefore, Reed and Pollock went to Cincinnati and obtained warrants for the arrest of the slaves and placed them in the hands of U.S. Marshal Lewis W. Sifford of the Southern District of Ohio. Sifford had been nominated for the position in 1857 by President James Buchanan, who was widely regarded as a "doughface"—a Northern man who favored the South.

Early on Thursday, September 20, 1860, Sifford undertook an expedition to arrest the three fugitives. He was accompanied by a posse of eight to ten special deputies, including his nephew, Deputy Marshal William Manson. Learning that the men they sought were hiding in three different houses, the posse divided into three parties so that they could surround each house. The plan was to simultaneously capture the wanted men. They also set a place to rendezvous afterward. While the houses were in the same vicinity, the distance between the first and the third was over a mile.

"It was dark when the parties started on their mission—three to the first house, four to the second, and three to the third, the latter being headed by [Marshal Sifford]," the *Anti-Slavery Bugle* reported.[325] Sifford's party succeeded in capturing their man. Following a circuitous route,

*Above*: The Fugitive Slave Law of 1850 served to encourage even more freedom seekers to head north. *Authors' collection.*

*Left*: A states' rights advocate, President James Buchanan felt the federal government should not interfere with slavery. *Library of Congress.*

they walked to a railroad station some fourteen to sixteen miles south of Iberia through a drenching rain. They were cold and tired by the time they reached their destination, so they obtained passage on a freight train to Columbus. They arrived back in Cincinnati on Friday evening. That night, Alexander Martin, the captive, was examined by U.S. Commissioner Edward Newhall, remanded into the custody of his owners and transported back to Kentucky.

However, the other two parties were not as successful. Those who had been detailed to the first house found when they entered it that their quarry had fled. "[A]s they were returning from the house they were met by several armed men who asked them where they had been. They answered that they were railroad men; and carrying a colored lantern, they were suffered to pass, and they immediately concealed themselves."[326] The party then hid themselves.

Meanwhile, those dispatched to the second house also found that the man they were hunting was not there. Two women quietly smoking pipes in the house laughed at them. As they left, they met a group of men, including one who resembled the man they were looking for. After seizing him, the posse members found themselves involved in an intense shootout that lasted about five minutes. One of the Black men had four fingers shot off his right hand while a white man took a bullet in the groin.

Two members of the first posse and one of the second fled to the rendezvous point, arriving at about the same time. Finding their courage, they decided they should go back to help their friends. As they approached the second house, one of them took cover in a fence corner while the other two continued on.

> *Two of the slave catchers were taken prisoners, had their arms taken from them, and their clothes considerably torn. They state that their money was also taken, and that a rope was procured to hang them, but abandoning this a platoon was drawn up to shoot them, but they were prevented by the interference of one of their party. They procured a pair of scissors and cut their hair off close to their scalps—lectured them on the evils of slave catching—set them free, and chased them with clubs and stones out of the neighborhood.*[327]

Eventually, the slave catchers reached the train and made their way home. There was a general expectation that the government in Washington would be seeking to punish the citizens of Iberia.

All that remains of Iberia College today is this Presbyterian Church. *Wikipedia photo by Nyttend.*

In December 1860, the grand jury for United States Court of the Northern District of Ohio at Cleveland handed down indictments for Reverend George Gordon, James Hammond, Avery (or Ashbury) Parker, Calvin Rowland (or Bowland), Joseph T. Baldwin, E.D. Asbury and Jonathan McLaren for obstructing U.S. Marshal Lewis Sifford while he was in the process of arresting a fugitive slave at Iberia on September 20, 1860. They, along with numerous others, were also charged with assaulting the slaves' owners and their assistants.

According to the *Holmes County Farmer*, "From common rumor it is known that a mob of fanatic Abolitionists, numbering about fifty persons, principally composed of the Students and Professors of Iberia College, led by the Rev. George Gordon, who has flew to parts unknown, rescued the prisoners, seized the officers of the United States and their assistants, stripped them of their clothing, cut off their hair, flogged and beat them most severely with rods and clubs, and drove them from the country."[328]

Marshal Johnson and his deputies—White and Given—went to Iberia for two days in search of the men indicted for rescuing the slaves. Instead, they arrested three others: Archibald Brownlee, Robert McLaren and Hiram Dunn. Reverend Gordon, it was learned, had fled to Canada.

President Abraham
Lincoln came to the
realization that the Union
could only be preserved
if slavery was abolished.
*Library of Congress.*

While Brownlee and McLaren posted bonds, Dunn was locked up in the Cleveland jail for, as the *Cleveland National Democrat* put it, "aggravated wickedness."[329]

Following their indictment, Brownlee, McLaren, Dunn and Gordon left the area. All but Gordon were arrested in January 1861. He eventually returned from Canada to face the music.

As the president of Iberia College, Gordon was recognized as the leader of the community and had largely directed the efforts to recover the captured slaves. Tried in December 1861, he was convicted, fined $300 (or perhaps $500) and sentenced to six months in jail for "obstructing the process" of the Fugitive Slave Law.[330]

After three months in prison, Gordon was pardoned by President Abraham Lincoln, but he would not accept it. To do so, he felt, implied guilt. But his health was declining due to the conditions in prison, and his family and friends prevailed on him to accept the presidential pardon. Finally, he did and went back to Iberia. He died six years later at the age of sixty-one.

# 12

# OH, HASTE ERE HE LEAVE US!

*Oh, haste, ere he leave us! for who will ride then,*
*For pleasure or gain, to the hunting of men?*
—*John Greenleaf Whittier, "The Hunters of Men"*

Slave catching was a cruel and heartless business, but William L. Manson seemed to relish it. Born in Frederick, Maryland, he grew up Lancaster, Ohio, where he worked as a teacher, salesman and town constable. According to a Kentucky history, "In 1854 he moved to Cincinnati, and was made a chief deputy under his uncle Lewis Sifford, then a United States marshal."[331] Manson would remain in that capacity throughout the administration of President James Buchanan and six months into President Abraham Lincoln's first term, before moving south to Kentucky. He was later appointed a justice of the peace, an office he held from 1868 to 1890.

At about eight or nine o'clock on the evening of Friday, October 12, 1860, up to a dozen or so kidnappers descended on two cabins at Mills Lot, a couple of miles outside Sandusky near the Lake Erie shore. They were led by Deputy Manson. Seven people of color were seized and dragged out of their homes—Henry Burns (or possibly Hutchins), his wife (a free Black woman) and one child and Thomas Marshall, his wife and two children.

The fugitives had come to the area the previous December, having fled from Mason County, Kentucky. After renting thirty acres of land, they erected the cabins and moved in around March. That spring, they cleared and planted seven acres of corn and other crops, enough to sustain them during the coming winter. Being so close to Canada, they likely felt safe.

Judging by the blood and other evidence of a scuffle, the victims had put up a ferocious fight. The *Anti-Slavery Bugle* reported: "A neighbor…heard Mrs. Hutchins crying, and asked what was the matter, when she replied that 'several persons were taking her away,' and called for help."[332] Grabbing a gun, the neighbor fired at a man who was attempting to hoist the woman over a fence. He fell to the ground, but others from the party rushed to his aid and carried the woman off. A seven-year-old child was later found in one of the cabins—either overlooked or intentionally left behind—as well as the trousers worn by one of the captured men.

"The Marshal and his company were hotly pursued" by the victims' neighbors, the *Cincinnati Gazette* reported, "but by the most adroit dodging through cornfields and woods, they escaped unharmed, and soon had the satisfaction of seeing the light of a train, which they stopped by swinging a red light, and got aboard."[333] It was the ten o'clock night train to Cincinnati on the Sandusky, Dayton & Cincinnati line.

The would-be rescuers had rushed to Castalia Station, but could not find the slave catchers in any of the railroad cars. Once the train started, however, "it was discovered that a dark car was attached, and that the kidnappers

Sometimes fugitives from slavery preferred death to being recaptured. *Authors' collection.*

and their victims had entered that car at Venice side-track, near where the assault had been committed, and not a regular place of stopping."[334]

Some suspicious-looking characters had visited the Venice siding earlier and told the railroad conductor—a man named Sherman—that they represented a group of eight hunters. They wanted to catch the train at the siding because they would be too tired to walk to the station. The conductor was also told that they would be joined by a party of detectives from Cincinnati and their "birds."[335] Sherman claimed the car "was put in the train by Superintendent Rice to go to Springfield. It was intended for our use, and was not warmed or lighted."[336]

After collecting the fares from Manson and the others, Sherman did not see them again. However, the men obtained a key from the brakeman and made use of the "dark car" for their own purposes. The *Cleveland Daily Leader* was adamant in demanding that the Ohio legislature take action to prohibit railroad employees from being "the active agents of Kentucky kidnappers and their still meaner Ohio official slave-hounds."[337]

Arriving in Cincinnati on Saturday, Manson hauled his prisoners before U.S. Commissioner Edward Newhall. Although the children and one of the women were free, all were remanded to Kentucky and a life of slavery. Only the seven-year-old girl and one other child escaped.

Two men passing through the area on Sunday morning near where the kidnapping had occurred chanced upon a two-and-a-half-year-old child partially wrapped in a sheet and concealed in a shock of corn. It had been there two nights and one day. "It was cold and swollen, and looked as though it had nearly cried itself to death."[338] Taken to a nearby house, the child soon recovered.

When Abraham Lincoln was elected president a month later on November 6, 1860, there were nearly four million enslaved people in the country. That was ten times the number in 1808, when the further importation of slaves into the United States was prohibited by Congress. The subsequent increase over the past half century was largely due to the high birth rate among slaves, some portion of which has been attributed to their systematic breeding for market, especially in Virginia, Maryland and Kentucky.[339] Exactly how much remains an open—and hotly debated—question. But in a slave household, there was generally one birth every three years, while in a white household there was one every four years.[340] As Thomas Jefferson observed, "A [slave] child raised every 2 years is of more profit than the crop of the best laboring man."[341]

African Americans celebrating the abolition of slavery in Washington, D.C. *Authors' collection.*

Another portion of the increase was due to smuggling, but again, the number of slaves brought into the country following the ban is also unknown. The bottom line was this: on the eve of the Civil War, the United States had more slaves than ever before, and many were finding their way to Ohio. The country was at a tipping point.

Then on December 18, 1860, South Carolina seceded from the Union. Although he declared it illegal, outgoing President Buchanan, an Andrew Jackson Democrat, took no action to stop it. His was strictly a hands-off administration, especially where slavery was concerned, leaving the states to sort things out for themselves. Three months later, the Civil War began.

Once the country was at war, the flow of fugitive slaves northward slowed down to a trickle. Sarah Lucy Bagby (or Bagbe) is often said to have been the last slave prosecuted under the Fugitive Slave Act. Born in Virginia in 1843, Lucy was purchased at the age of nine by John Goshorn of Wheeling, [West] Virginia, for $600. Five years later, he presented her to his son, William S. Goshorn, as a gift.

On or about October 17, 1860, Lucy accompanied William's daughter to Beaver, Pennsylvania—or so she said. However, she had actually taken advantage of Goshorn's absence from home "to escape north via the Underground Railroad by the Ohio River to Beaver, Pennsylvania, before moving on to Pittsburgh."[342] Making her way to Cleveland, Lucy was given shelter by the family of William E. Ambush—chairman of the Fugitive Aid Society. She then found employment with the family of George A. Benedict.

In January 1861, the Goshorns managed to locate Lucy, possibly due to the betrayal of a Black woman. After they swore out a warrant, U.S. Marshal Seth A. Abbey took the runaway into custody at the home of Lucius A. Benton, where she had been working for a couple of weeks. Colonel Abbey, who was accompanied by William Goshorn, Deputy Marshal J.H. Johnson and Lambert White, placed the young woman in the county jail.

Lucy's friends immediately engaged Rufus P. Spalding as her legal counsel. A leader in the establishment of the Ohio Republican Party, Spalding obtained a writ of habeas corpus issued by Probate Court Judge Daniel R. Tilden, removing her from Abbey's custody and placing her in Sheriff Craw's. Tilden was Spalding's law partner.

Just before the hearing was to commence on January 21, 1861, Ambush and Goshorn exchanged words and then drew their pistols. Fortunately, "they were prevented from firing by the interposition of people in the Court room."[343] Outside, a crowd of people, both Black and white and some armed with knives, milled about. Although there were several skirmishes, no one was seriously injured. Rumors that an attempt would be made to rescue Lucy came to naught.

Spalding argued that the Fugitive Slave Act was unconstitutional and immoral—but to no avail. At the hearing's conclusion, U.S. Judge Taylor ordered Lucy remanded back to her owner. Although the Republicans of Cleveland had provided her with three attorneys, *The Liberator* branded her defense a "sham."[344]

The Goshorns immediately returned Lucy to Wheeling by train "where she was placed in jail and severely punished."[345] A message from the Goshorns was later published in the *Cleveland Herald*, expressing their gratitude to the city's citizens for their kindness and for shielding them "from the insults of your colored population."[346]

Two years later, following the Emancipation Proclamation, Lucy walked to Pittsburgh. She subsequently married George Johnson and moved to Cleveland, where she worked as a cook and servant. Lucy passed away in July 1906. Her tombstone bears the legend, "Unfettered and Free."

When the South lost the Civil War, some white supremacist groups turned to terrorism. *Library of Congress.*

Although the incident received little attention, George Lee may have actually been the last fugitive slave to be remanded to his owner, leastways from Ohio. The legal property of David Morrison, a farmer residing near Clarksburg, [West] Virginia, Lee, age twenty-five, had been hired out to Morrison's son in St. Louis, Missouri, two years earlier. Sometime afterward, he fled to Cincinnati, where he secured a job as a porter at the Southgate House. He was described as "intelligent and active, though somewhat lame."[347]

On April 3, 1861, Lee was arrested by U.S. Marshal Lewis W. Sifford. The uncle of William Manson, Sifford was born in Maryland and moved to Ross County, Ohio, as a young man. In addition to operating a sawmill, he served as a county commissioner and as a representative in the state legislature. However, it was likely his "imposing appearance" that was most germane to his duties as a marshal.

According to the *Cincinnati Gazette*, Lee "was taken without opposition before Commissioner [Edward] Newhall, and on the testimony of Mr. Bartlett, of Covington, and two sons of the claimant, he was remanded to slavery."[348] Confined across the river in the Covington jail, Lee was transported back to Clarksburg the next day. Not long afterward, Sifford resigned his office and became the resident engineer of the Ohio Canal Company.

Nine days later, on April 12, the Civil War began when Confederate troops fired on Union soldiers at Fort Sumter, South Carolina. President Lincoln had barely taken office. For all intents and purposes, the era of slave catchers prowling the free states of the North was over, but slavery—the institution itself—would persist until the war came to an end four years later. Meanwhile, the long struggle for racial equality was just beginning.

# NOTES

## Introduction

1. Hagedorn, *Beyond the River.*
2. Native Americans were also subject to being enslaved by colonists, although they exhibited greater moral ambivalence about doing so.
3. Kahn and Bouie, "Atlantic Slave Trade in Two Minutes."
4. Per the Global Slavery Index, the number of currently enslaved people exceeds forty million.
5. Gairdner, *Trouble with Canada.*
6. The Spanish brought as many as one hundred African slaves to "La Florida" in 1526.
7. "Massachusetts Body of Liberties."
8. "Northwest Ordinance (1787)."
9. Ibid.
10. Heritage Guide to the Constitution, "Fugitive Slave Clause."
11. Many Black slave owners purchased their spouses or children for humanitarian reasons, but there were some who did so strictly for their own economic benefit and control.
12. House Divided Project, "Dickinson and Slavery."
13. Siebert, "Major E.C. Dawes and Mr. Ealy."
14. Phillips, *Slave Economy of the Old South.* Phillips's legacy as a historian is problematic. While some of his peers feel he was proslavery, others accept his denial of the charge. Still few question the value of his pioneering work on the topic.

## 1. The Hunting of Men

15. Whittier, whom Nathaniel Hawthorne described in jest as "a fiery Quaker youth, to whom the muse has perversely assigned a battle-trumpet," devoted twenty years of his life and two volumes of poetry to the abolitionist cause.
16. Calhoun had defended slavery as the "peculiar domestick institution" in 1830.
17. Du Bois, *Black Folk Then and Now.*
18. Melish, *Melish's Travels through the United States of America.*
19. Ibid.
20. Ibid.
21. de Tocqueville, *Democracy in America.*
22. Massie, *Nathaniel Massie.*
23. Ibid.
24. Ibid.
25. Meyers and Walker, *Historic Black Settlements of Ohio.*
26. Author Sherman Alexie, who grew up on a reservation, prefers the term *Indians* to *Native Americans.*
27. Pocock, "Slavery and Freedom in the Early Republic."
28. Ibid.
29. Ibid.
30. Ibid.
31. Meyers and Walker, *Historic Black Settlements of Ohio.*
32. Smith, "First Fugitive Slave Case of Record in Ohio."
33. The equivalent of $7,270 in 2021.
34. Smith, "First Fugitive Slave Case of Record in Ohio."
35. Smith, *Political History of Slavery.*
36. Ibid.
37. Basler, *Collected Works of Abraham Lincoln.*

## 2. The Lords of Our Land

38. Although Clay spoke out against slavery, he was enamored of the personal benefits and status of having slaves.
39. Finkelman, *Imperfect Union.*
40. Supreme Court of Ohio and the Ohio Judicial System, "John McLean."
41. Randolph, *Reports of Cases Argued.*

42. Ibid.

43. Ibid.

44. Ibid.

45. Ibid.

46. Desha had earlier pardoned his own son on a murder charge.

47. Alilunas, "Fugitive Slave Cases."

48. Hammond, *Cases Decided in the Supreme Court of Ohio.*

49. Howe, *Historical Collections of Ohio.*

50. Meyers and Walker, *Lynching and Mob Violence in Ohio.*

51. Taylor, *Frontiers of Freedom.*

52. *Delaware Register or Farmers', Manufacturers' and Mechanics Advocate*, August 15, 1829.

53. Taylor, "Reconsidering the 'Forced' Exodus of 1829."

54. An octoroon, by definition, had one great-grandparent who was African, the rest European (Birney, *James G. Birney and His Times*).

55. Ibid.

56. Ibid.

57. Ibid.

58. History, "Salmon P. Chase."

59. Carson, *History of the Supreme Court of the United States.*

60. Birney, *James G. Birney and His Times.*

61. Ibid.

62. Trowbridge, *Ferry Boy and the Financier.*

63. Carson, *History of the Supreme Court of the United States.*

64. Hammond, *Cases Decided in the Supreme Court of Ohio.*

65. Alilunas, "Fugitive Slave Cases."

## 3. Though Hundreds Are Caught

66. Hylton, "Before There Were 'Red' and 'Blue' States."

67. Clymer, *Family Money.*

68. Now known as the Supreme Court of Mississippi.

69. "Slave Case," *The Liberator* (Boston, MA).

70. Anderson and Anderson, *Life and Letters of Judge Thomas J. Anderson.*

71. Jacob, *History of Marion County.*

72. Winter, *History of Northwest Ohio.*

73. Ibid.

74. Middleton, *Black Laws.*

75. Ibid.
76. Niven, *Salmon P. Chase*.
77. "$50 Reward," *Cincinnati (OH) Enquirer*.
78. "Mob in Cincinnati," *The Liberator* (Boston, MA).
79. Ibid.
80. Ibid.
81. Ibid.
82. Ibid.
83. Ibid.
84. One of the *Amistad* survivors, a child named Margru, later studied at Oberlin College.
85. "Abolition in Cincinnati," *The Evening Post* (New York).
86. Taylor, *Frontiers of Freedom*.

## 4. So Speed to Their Hunting

87. Wright, "Station on the Underground Railroad."
88. Ibid.
89. "Ohio and Slavery," *Anti-Slavery Bugle* (New Lisbon, OH).
90. Ibid.
91. Ibid.
92. "Slave Decision," *American Citizen* (Canton, MS).
93. "Abduction Case," *Democrat and Herald* (Wilmington, OH).
94. "Western Law," *Niles National Register* (St. Louis, MO).
95. "Abduction Case."
96. Ibid.
97. Middleton, *Black Laws*.
98. "Western Law."
99. The case was never published.
100. "No Slavery in Ohio," *Niles National Register* (St. Louis, MO).
101. "Slave Decision."
102. Campbell, *Slave Catchers*.
103. Ibid.
104. "Salmon Portland Chase," *Ohio Law Reporter*.
105. Ibid.
106. Greve, *Centennial History of Cincinnati*.
107. Trowbridge, *Ferry Boy and the Financier*.
108. Ibid.

109. Ibid.
110. "Salmon Portland Chase."
111. Greve, *Centennial History of Cincinnati*.
112. Trowbridge, *Ferry Boy and the Financier*.
113. Greve, *Centennial History of Cincinnati*.
114. Ibid.
115. Trowbridge, *Ferry Boy and the Financier*.
116. Ibid.
117. "Samuel Watson," *Green-Mountain Freeman* (Montpelier, VT).
118. Greve, *Centennial History of Cincinnati*.
119. "Samuel Watson."
120. Ibid.
121. Ibid.
122. Ibid.
123. Chase, *Address and Reply on the Presentation of a Testimonial to S.P. Chase*.
124. Meigs, "Judges Supreme Court State of Ohio."

## 5. Gay Luck to Our Hunters

125. "Driskell v. Parish," *Western Law Journal*.
126. Beecher became blind in 1831 but later recovered enough of his sight that he could continue to practice law with the aid of his wife, Jane Turk Beecher, who read and wrote for him.
127. "Boys Claimed as Fugitive Slaves," *Sandusky (OH) Clarion*.
128. Ibid.
129. Ibid.
130. Sloane, "Underground Railroad of the Firelands."
131. Peeke, *Standard History of Erie County*.
132. Ibid.
133. Walker, *Western Law Journal*.
134. Trowbridge, *Ferry Boy and the Financier*.
135. "Kidnappers," *Anti-Slavery Bugle (New Lisbon, OH)*.
136. Three years later, Wingate was elected vice president (Henry Clay was president) of the first antislavery convention held in Kentucky.
137. Swan is best remembered as the author of many reference books on Ohio jurisprudence.
138. Lee, *History of the City of Columbus*.
139. "Kidnapping! Dating Outrage!" *Huron (Oh) Reflector*.

140. Ibid.
141. Taylor, *Centennial History of Columbus and Franklin County*.
142. Lee, *History of the City of Columbus*.
143. Walker, *Western Law Journal*, vol. 3.
144. Much of the genealogical work was pieced together from Hamlin, *They Went Thataway*, and Brannon, *Long Journey West*.
145. "Other Side," *Portage (OH) Sentinel*.
146. Morehead would be elected to Congress two years later and became governor of Kentucky after that.
147. Lee, *History of the City of Columbus*.
148. Finney purportedly stood trial in Dayton a few years before in which he established his freedom, but this has not been verified.
149. "Kidnappers," *Anti-Slavery Bugle* (New Lisbon, OH).
150. Ibid.
151. Ibid.
152. Dennison would become the twenty-fourth governor of Ohio (1860–62), while Swayne would become a justice of the U.S. Supreme Court (1862–81), replacing his friend John McLean.
153. *History of Franklin and Pickaway Counties*.
154. Lee, *History of the City of Columbus*.
155. "Important Decision," *Anti-Slavery Bugle* (New Lisbon, OH).
156. "Jerry Phinney," *Anti-Slavery Bugle* (New Lisbon, OH).

## 6. The Saint and the Sinner

157. Crenshaw, *Bury Me in a Free Land*.
158. Meyers and Walker, *Historic Black Settlements of Ohio*.
159. Hale, "Famous Negro Polley Family of Lawrence County."
160. Crigler, "Justice for Former Slaves 162 Years Later."
161. "Kidnapping Case," *New York Tribune*.
162. Wells, *Blind No More*.
163. *Ohio State Journal*, June 28, 1850.
164. "Kidnapping Case."
165. Middleton, *Black Laws*.
166. "Gov. Dennison's Message Relating to the Polly Negro Family," *Ironton (OH) Register*.
167. *Burlington (VT) Free Press*, November 13, 1851.
168. "Case of Polly Negroes Memorandum," Peyton Polly Collection.

169. "Ralph Seete to Governor Salmon P. Chase, July 25, 1856," Peyton Polly Collection.
170. Middleton, *Black Laws*.
171. "Ralph Seete to A.M. Gangener, November 25, 1859," Peyton Polly Collection.
172. Cox, "Jugbands of Louisville."
173. Ibid.
174. Ibid.
175. Clarke, *Narratives of the Sufferings of Lewis and Milton Clarke*.
176. Malden or Fort Malden was a former township in Ontario that is now part of Amherstburg.
177. Clarke, *Narratives of the Sufferings of Lewis and Milton Clarke*.
178. Cox, Randolph and Harris, "Jugbands of Louisville."
179. "Important Slave Case Decision," *Louisville (KY) Daily Courier*.
180. "Fugitive Slave Case," *Zanesville (OH) Courier*.
181. "Fugitive Slave Case in Cincinnati," *Anti-Slavery Bugle* (New Lisbon, OH).
182. "Fugitive Slave Case."
183. Ibid.
184. "Fugitive Slave Case in Cincinnati," *Anti-Slavery Bugle* (New Lisbon, OH).
185. Ibid.

## 7. This Home of the Free

186. Uncle Tom is presented as a "noble hero" who stands up for his beliefs. The use of the term as a racial epithet owes more to the character as he was portrayed in subsequent stage productions than in the context of the novel.
187. Greve, *Centennial History of Cincinnati*.
188. Two years later, Commissioner Carpenter would resign in protest of the Fugitive Slave Act.
189. Coffin, *Reminiscences of Levi Coffin*.
190. Greve, *Centennial History of Cincinnati*.
191. "Miller v. McQuerry," https://law.resource.org/pub/us/case/reporter/F.Cas/0017.f.cas/0017.f.cas.0335.pdf.
192. Greve, *Centennial History of Cincinnati*.
193. "Fugitive Slave Case," *Gallipolis (OH) Journal*.
194. Greve, *Centennial History of Cincinnati*.
195. In his autobiography, Reverend William Troy described an incident that took place in 1852, involving three slaves who arrived in Cincinnati

aboard the steamboat *Baltic*. However, it so closely resembles this one that it appears he was in error.

196. Troy, *Hair-Breadth Escapes from Slavery to Freedom*.

197. "Three Slaves Taken by Habeas Corpus," *Cincinnati (OH) Gazette*.

198. Ibid.

199. Troy, *Hair-Breadth Escapes From Slavery to Freedom*.

200. Sloane, "Underground Railroad of the Firelands."

201. "Fugitive Slave Case in Cincinnati," *Louisville (KY) Daily Courier*.

202. Ibid.

203. Meyers and Walker, *Lynching and Mob Violence in Ohio*.

204. A Republican, Hayes would become president of the United States in 1877.

205. Coffin, *Reminiscences of Levi Coffin*.

206. "Fugitive Slave Case in Cincinnati."

207. Greve, *Centennial History of Cincinnati*.

208. "Escape of an Alleged Fugitive," *The Liberator* (Boston).

209. "Fugitive Slave Case," *Richmond (VA) Dispatch*.

210. Troy, *Hair-Breadth Escapes from Slavery to Freedom*.

211. Coffin, *Reminiscences of Levi Coffin*.

212. Troy, *Hair-Breadth Escapes from Slavery to Freedom*.

213. Coffin, *Reminiscences of Levi Coffin*.

214. Troy, *Hair-Breadth Escapes from Slavery to Freedom*.

215. Reverend William M. Mitchell wrote that he also assisted in this subterfuge (Mitchell, *Under-Ground Railroad*).

216. Troy, *Hair-Breadth Escapes from Slavery to Freedom*.

217. Coffin, *Reminiscences of Levi Coffin*.

218. Ibid.

219. Greve, *Centennial History of Cincinnati*.

220. "Honor to Whom Honor Is Due," *Weekly Marysville (OH) Tribune*.

## 8. Right Merrily Hunting

221. "Look-out Slaveholders," *Hillsdale (MI) Standard*.

222. Ibid.

223. Obviously, calling an adult male "boy" reinforced the inequality of their relationship.

224. Ibid.

225. "Preventing Escape of Slaves and the Recovery of Fugitives," *Anti-Slavery Bugle* (New Lisbon, OH).

226. "Underground Railroad," *The Republic* (Washington, D.C.).

227. Douglas became a slaveholder through marriage and used the income to further his political aspirations.

228. Commissioner Pendery evidently owed his job to Supreme Court Justice John McLean, whose wife was Pendery's sister-in-law.

229. "Arrest and Examination of Eight Fugitive Slaves in Cincinnati," *New York Herald*.

230. Ibid.

231. Ibid.

232. "Rev. Henry Dennison's Slave Girl," *The National Era* (Washingon, D.C.).

233. Lee, *History of the City of Columbus*.

234. "Slave Case—Another Triumph of Freedom," *Anti-Slavery Bugle* (New Lisbon, OH).

235. "Good for Rosetta," *Anti-Slavery Bugle* (New Lisbon, OH).

236. "Slave Case—Another Triumph of Freedom," *Anti-Slavery Bugle* (New Lisbon, OH).

237. Ibid.

238. Lee, *History of the City of Columbus*.

239. Greve, *Centennial History of Cincinnati*.

240. In 1858, Reverend Denison died of the flu at the age of thirty-six.

241. "Good for Rosetta," *Anti-Slavery Bugle* (New Lisbon, OH).

242. Lee, *History of the City of Columbus*.

243. Greve, *Centennial History of Cincinnati*.

244. Coffin, *Reminiscences of Levi Coffin*. .

245. Trowbridge, *Ferry Boy and the Financier*.

246. "Fugitive Slave Case," *Cincinnati (OH) Enquirer*.

247. "Fugitive Case," *Carroll (OH) Free Press*.

248. Howe, *Historical Collections of Ohio*.

249. Trowbridge, *Ferry Boy and the Financier*.

250. Ibid.

251. Ibid.

## 9. And Woman, Kind Woman

252. "Real Justice Taney," *Wilson Quarterly*.

253. "No Rights Which the White Man Was Bound to Respect," American Constitution Society for Law and Policy.

254. Stafford, "Clark County Sheriff Was Felled."

255. Ware, *History of Mechanicsburg, Ohio.*
256. That was two hundred more than Harriet Tubman claimed.
257. Ware, *History of Mechanicsburg, Ohio.*
258. Ibid.
259. Ibid.
260. "Fugitive Slave Case," *Evansville (IN) Daily Journal.*
261. "Cases Arising Out of the Slave Rescue in Ohio," *Baltimore (MD) Sun.*
262. Ware, *History of Mechanicsburg, Ohio.*
263. Tyler, *Memoir of Roger Brooke Taney.*
264. "Another Fugitive Slave Case," *Eaton (OH) Democrat.*
265. Ibid.
266. Ibid.
267. "Trial of Wm. M. Connelly," *Randolph Journal* (Winchester, IN).
268. Ibid.
269. Ibid.
270. Greve, *Centennial History of Cincinnati.*
271. Ibid.
272. Cochran, "Oberlin-Wellington Rescue Case."
273. Kornblith, *Elusive Utopia.*
274. Cochran, "Oberlin-Wellington Rescue Case."
275. Ibid.
276. Kornblith, *Elusive Utopia.*
277. Boynton had the honorific title of brigadier general of the Second Brigade, Ninth Division of the Ohio State Militia.
278. May, *Fugitive Slave Law and Its Victims.*
279. Neff, *Bench and Bar of Northern Ohio.*
280. Cochran, "Oberlin-Wellington Rescue Case."
281. Ibid.
282. May, *Fugitive Slave Law and Its Victims.*
283. Cochran, "Oberlin-Wellington Rescue Case."
284. Ibid.
285. Copeland and another Black man who aided in the slave rescue, Lewis Sheridan Leary, later joined John Brown's raid on Harpers Ferry.
286. "Charles Langston's Speech," https://www2.oberlin.edu/external/EOG/Oberlin-Wellington_Rescue/c._langston_speech.htm.
287. Neff, *Bench and Bar of Northern Ohio.*
288. "Return of Mr. Welton," *Summit County (OH) Beacon.*

## 10. The Parson Has Turned

289. "Arrest of a Fugitive Slave," *Daily Press* (Cincinnati, OH).
290. Ibid.
291. Ibid.
292. "Another Fugitive Slave Case," *The Liberator*(Boston, MA).
293. Ibid.
294. "More Fugitive Slave Excitement," *Buffalo (NY) Daily Courier.*
295. "Fugitive Slave Case," *Holmes County (OH) Republican.*
296. "Fugitive Slave Case in Zanesville," *New York Tribune.*
297. "Late Fugitive Slave Case at Zanesville, Ohio," *Detroit (MI) Free Press.*
298. "Another Slave Case," *Fremont (OH) Weekly Journal.*
299. "Fugitive Slave Case."
300. "Fugitive Slave Law," *Prairie News* (Okolona, MS).
301. "Modern Inquisition," *Brooklyn (NY) Daily Eagle.*
302. "More Rescue Trials," *Anti-Slavery Bugle* (New Lisbon, OH).
303. "Fugitive-Slave Case," *Cincinnati (OH) Enquirer.*
304. "Fugitive Slave Arrest at Columbus, Ohio," *Baltimore (MD) Sun.*
305. Ibid.
306. White would later be chief justice of the Ohio Supreme Court.
307. "Kidnapping at Columbus," *Holmes County (OH) Republican.*
308. Ibid.
309. Ibid.
310. "Free Negro Sold as a Slave," *Anti-Slavery Bugle* (New Lisbon, OH).
311. Du Bois, *John Brown.*

## 11. The Home of the White

312. "Waggoner Kidnapping Case," *Cincinnati (OH) Daily Press.*
313. "Negro-Philanthropy," *Cincinnati (OH) Daily Press.*
314. "Is This a Civilized County?" *Pomeroy (OH) Weekly Telegraph.*
315. "Negro-Philanthropy."
316. "Is This a Civilized County?" *Pomeroy (OH) Weekly Telegraph.*
317. "Decision in the Waggoner Case Yesterday," *Cincinnati (OH) Daily Press.*
318. May, *Fugitive Slave Law and Its Victims.*
319. "[Communicated.]," *Cincinnati (OH) Daily Press.*
320. "Decision in the Waggoner Case Yesterday."
321. "Case of Charles Waggoner," *The Liberator* (Boston, MA).

NOTES TO PAGES 146–157

322. "Circuit Court—Fourth Day—Decision in the Waggoner Case," *Anti-Slavery Bugle* (New Lisbon, OH).
323. "End of the Waggoner Case," *Cincinnati (OH) Daily Press*.
324. He was not the Colonel George P. Webster who died in the Battle of Perrysville, Kentucky, in 1862.
325. "Attempt to Capture Bracken County Slaves," *Randolph Journal* (Winchester, IN).
326. "Late Kidnapping Case," *Anti-Slavery Bugle* (New Lisbon, OH).
327. Ibid.
328. "Iberia Outrage," *Holmes County (OH) Farmer*.
329. May, *Fugitive Slave Law and Its Victims*.
330. "Remarks of Rev. George Gordon to the U.S. Court," *Holmes (OH) Republican*.

# 12. Oh, Haste Ere He Leave Us!

331. Connelley, *History of Kentucky*.
332. "Last Negro Hunt in Ohio," *Anti-Slavery Bugle* (New Lisbon, OH).
333. "Another Exploit of U.S. Deputy Marshal Manson," *Cleveland (OH) Daily Leader*.
334. Ibid.
335. "Last Negro Hunt in Ohio."
336. "Kidnapping Case—Conductor Sherman," *Cleveland (OH) Morning Leader*.
337. "Another Exploit of U.S. Deputy Marshal Manson.
338. "Sandusky Kidnapping Case," *Cleveland (OH) Daily Leader*.
339. Theodore Parker, a Massachusetts abolitionist, referred to the practice of breeding slaves in a letter published on January 17, 1848, in *The National Era*.
340. Birth rates were much lower in Brazil and the British Caribbean due to such factors as harsher working conditions and higher mortality. The slaveholders also believed it was cheaper to buy replacement slaves than to rear their children.
341. "Extract from Thomas Jefferson to Joel Yancey," Jefferson Quotes & Family Letters.
342. Day and Wickens, "Arrest and Trial of Lucy Bagby."
343. Malvin, *Into Freedom*.
344. "Human Sacrifice!" *The Liberator*, (Boston, MA).
345. Malvin, *Into Freedom*.

346. "Biography: Sara Lucy Bagby," *Ohio County Public Library*.
347. "Remanding of a Fugitive Slave," *Cincinnati (OH) Enquirer*.
348. Ibid.

# BIBLIOGRAPHY

*Books*

Anderson, Thomas Jefferson, and Nancy Dunlevy Anderson. *Life and Letters of Judge Thomas J. Anderson and Wife*. Columbus, OH: F.J. Heer, 1904.

Basler, Roy P., ed. *Collected Works of Abraham Lincoln*. New Brunswick, NJ: Rutgers University Press, 1953.

Birney, William. *James G. Birney and His Times*: New York: D. Appleton and Company, 1890.

Brannon, Janice Lee. *The Long Journey West*. Self-published, 2013.

Campbell, Stanley W. *The Slave Catchers: Enforcement of the Fugitive Slave Law, 1850–1860*. New York: W.W. Norton, 1971.

Carson, Hampton Lawrence. *The History of the Supreme Court of the United States*. Philadelphia, PA: F.W. Ziegler Company, 1904.

Chase, Salmon P. *The Address and Reply on the Presentation of a Testimonial to S.P. Chase*. Cincinnati, OH: H.W. Derby & Company, 1845.

Clarke, Lewis. *Narratives of the Sufferings of Lewis and Milton Clarke*. Boston: Bela Marsh, 1846.

Clymer, Jeffery. *Family Money: Property, Race, and Literature in the Nineteenth Century*. New York: Oxford University Press, 2013.

Coffin, Levi. *Reminiscences of Levi Coffin*. Cincinnati, OH: Western Tract Society, 1876.

Connelley, William Elsey, and E.M. Coulter. *History of Kentucky*. Chicago: American Historical Society, 1922.

de Tocqueville, Alexis. *Democracy in America*. New York: George Dearborn & Company, 1835.

Dickinson, Cornelius Evarts. *A History of Belpre, Washington County, Ohio*. Parkersburg, WV: Globe Printing & Binding Company, 1920.

Du Bois, W.E.B. *Black Folk Then and Now*. New York: Oxford University Press, 2007.

———. *John Brown*. New York: Routledge, 2015.

Finkelman, Paul. *An Imperfect Union: Slavery, Federalism, and Comity*. Union, NJ: Lawbook Exchange, 2000.

Gairdner, William D. *The Trouble with Canada…Still!* Toronto: BPS Books, 2011.

Gilmer, Francis W. *Reports of Cases Decided in the Court of Appeals of Virginia, From April 10th 1820, to June 28th 1821*. Richmond, VA: Franklin Press, 1821.

Greenberg, Kenneth S., ed. *The Confessions of Nat Turner and Related Documents*. New York: St. Martins Press, 1997.

Greve, Charles Theodore. *Centennial History of Cincinnati and Representative Citizens*. Chicago: Biographical Publishing Company, 1904.

Griffler, Keith P. *Front Line of Freedom*. Lexington: University Press of Kentucky, 2004.

Hagedorn, Ann. *Beyond the River: The Untold Story of the Heroes of the Underground Railroad*. New York: Simon & Schuster, 2002.

Hamlin, Charles Hughes. *They Went Thataway*. Baltimore, MD: Clearfield Company, 2007.

Hammond, Charles. *Cases Decided in the Supreme Court of Ohio. December, 1827 and December, 1828*. Vol. 3. Cincinnati, OH: Robert Clarke & Company, 1887.

———. *Cases Decided in the Supreme Court of Ohio in Bank*. Vol. 7. Cincinnati, OH: Robert Clarke & Company, 1887.

*History of Franklin and Pickaway Counties, Ohio*. Cleveland, OH: Williams Brothers, 1880.

Howe, Henry. *Historical Collections of Ohio*. Cincinnati, OH: G.J. Krehbiel & Company, 1902.

Jacob, J. Wilbur. *History of Marion County, Ohio and Representative Citizens*. Marion, OH: 1907.

Knepp, Gary L. *Freedom's Struggle: A Response to Slavery from the Ohio Borderlands*. Milford, OH: Little Miami Publishing, 2008.

Kornblith, Gary J., and Carol Lasser. *Elusive Utopia*. Baton Rouge: Louisiana State University Press, 2018.

Lane, Samuel A. *Fifty Years and Over of Akron and Summit County*. Akron, OH: Beacon Job Department, 1892.

Lee, Alfred Emory. *History of the City of Columbus, Capital of Ohio*. New York: Munsell & Company, 1892.

Malvin, John North. *Into Freedom: The Autobiography of John Malvin, Free Negro, 1795–1880*. Cleveland, OH: Press of Western Reserve University, 1966.

Massie, David Meade. *Nathaniel Massie, a Pioneer of Ohio*. Cincinnati, OH: Robert Clarke Company, 1896.

May, Samuel. *The Fugitive Slave Law and Its Victims*. New York: American Anti-Slavery Society, 1861.

Melish, John. *Melish's Travels through the United States of America*. Carlisle, MA: Applewood Books, 1812.

Meyers, David. *A Glance of Heaven: The Design and Operation of the Separatist Society of Zoar*. Columbus, OH: Exploding Stove Media, 2015.

Meyers, David, and Elise Meyers Walker. *Historic Black Settlements of Ohio*. Charleston, SC: The History Press, 2020.

———. *Lynching and Mob Violence in Ohio*. Jefferson, NC: McFarland & Company, 2018.

Middleton, Stephen. *The Black Laws: Race and the Legal Process in Early Ohio*. Athens: Ohio University Press 2005.

Mitchell, W.M. *The Under-Ground Railroad*. Birmingham, UK: Richard Priddy, 1860.

Neff, William B. *Bench and Bar of Northern Ohio*. Cleveland, OH: Historical Publishing Company, 1921.

Niven, John. *Salmon P. Chase. A Biography*. New York: Oxford University Press, 1995.

Peeke, Hewson L. *A Standard History of Erie County, Ohio*. Chicago: Lewis Publishing Company, 1916.

Perrin, William Henry, ed. *History of Stark County: With an Outline Sketch of Ohio*. Chicago: Baskin & Battey 1881.

Phillips, Ulrich Bonnell. *The Slave Economy of the Old South*. Baton Rouge: Louisiana State University Press, 1986.

Randolph, Peyton. *Reports of Cases Argued and Determined in the Court of Appeals of Virginia*. Richmond, VA: Peter Cottom, 1823.

Riddell, William Renwick. *The Slave in Canada*. Washington, D.C.: Association for the Study of Negro Life and History, 1820.

Siebert, Wilbur Henry, *Mysteries of Ohio's Underground Railroad*. Columbus, OH: Long's College Book Company, 1951.

Smith, William Henry. *A Political History of Slavery*. New York: G.P. Putnam's Sons, 1903.

Soodalter, Ron. *Hanging Captain Gordon: The Life and Times of An American Slave Trader*. New York: Washington Square Press, 2007.

Sowell, Thomas. *The Thomas Sowell Reader*. New York: Basic Books, 2011.

Taylor, Nikki Marie. *Frontiers of Freedom: Cincinnati's Black Community, 1802–1868*. Athens: Ohio University Press, 2005.

Taylor, William Alexander. *Centennial History of Columbus and Franklin County, Ohio*. Chicago: S.J. Clarke Publishing Company 1909.

Trowbridge, John Townsend. *The Ferry Boy and the Financier*. Boston: Walker, Wise & Company, 1864.

Troy, Reverend William. *Hair-Breadth Escapes from Slavery to Freedom*. Manchester, UK: Guardian Steam-Printing Offices, 1861.

Tyler, Samuel. *Memoir of Roger Brooke Taney, L.L.D.* Baltimore, MD: John Murphy & Company, 1876.

Walker, T., ed. *The Western Law Journal*, Vol. 3. *October 1845–October 1846*. Cincinnati, OH: J.F. Desilver, 1846.

Walker, T., C.D. Coffin and C. Gilman, editors. *The Western Law Journal*. Vol. 5. Cincinnati, OH: J.F. Desilver, 1848.

Ware, Joseph. *History of Mechanicsburg, Ohio*. Columbus, OH F.J. Heer Printing Company, 1917.

Wells, Jonathan Daniel. *Blind No More: African American Resistance, Free-Soil Politics, and the Coming of the Civil War*. Athens: University of Georgia Press, 2019.

Winter, Nevin Otto. *A History of Northwest Ohio*. Chicago: Lewis Publishing Company, 1917.

## *Articles and Other*

Alilunas, Leo. "Fugitive Slave Cases in Ohio Prior to 1850." *Ohio State Archaeological and Historical Quarterly* 49, no. 2 (April–June 1940).

*American Citizen* (Canton, MS). "The Slave Decision." June 12, 1841.

American Constitution Society for Law and Policy. "No Rights Which the White Man was Bound to Respect." Accessed June 29, 2018. https://www. acslaw.org/acsblog/no-rights-which-the-white-man-was-bound-to-respect.

*Anti-Slavery Bugle* (New Lisbon, OH). "The Cleveland Kidnapping Case." November 19, 1859.

———. "Circuit Court—Fourth Day—Decision in the Waggoner Case." August 25, 1860.

———. "Excitement at Washington Ohio." July 21, 1860.

———. "A Free Negro Sold as a Slave." January 14, 1860.

————. "Fugitive Slave Case in Cincinnati." March 1, 1851.

————. "Good for Rosetta." May 5, 1855.

————. "Important Decision." February 5, 1847.

————. "Jerry Phinney." April 24, 1846.

————. "The Kidnappers." April 24, 1846.

————. "Kidnapping at Akron." May 27, 1854.

————. "The Last Negro Hunt in Ohio." October 27, 1860.

————. "The Late Kidnapping Case." October 6, 1860.

————. "More of the Washington Kidnapping Affair." August 25, 1860.

————. "More Rescue Trials." May 28, 1859.

————. "Ohio and Slavery." September 16, 1854.

————. "Preventing Escape of Slaves and the Recovery of Fugitives." December 18, 1852.

————. "A Slave Case—Another Triumph of Freedom." March 24, 1855.

*Baltimore (MD) Sun.* "The Cases Arising Out of the Slave Rescue in Ohio." July 13, 1857.

————. "The Fugitive Slave Arrest at Columbus, Ohio." November 2, 1859.

*Brooklyn (NY) Daily Eagle.* "The Modern Inquisition." June 23, 1859.

Bryant, Brooks, and Emily Brammer. "The Fee Brothers." *Clio: Your Guide to History.* July 24, 2018. Accessed August 27, 2019. https://www.theclio.com/entry/11368.

*Buffalo (NY) Daily Courier.* "More Fugitive Slave Excitement." March 30, 1859.

*Burlington (VT) Free Press.* November 13, 1851.

*Carroll Free Press* (Carrollton, OH). "The Fugitive Case." February 21, 1856.

"Charles Langston's Speech." https://www2.oberlin.edu/external/EOG/Oberlin-Wellington_Rescue/c._langston_speech.htm. Accessed July 11, 2020.

*Cincinnati (OH) Commercial.* "Another Fugitive Slave Remanded to Bondage." November 14, 1859.

*Cincinnati (OH) Daily Press.* "Arrest of a Fugitive Slave." March 26, 1859.

————. "[Communicated.]" June 7, 1860.

————. "Decision in the Waggoner Case Yesterday." June 5, 1860.

————. "The End of the Waggoner Case." August 17, 1860.

————. "Negro-Philanthropy." May 25, 1860.

————. "The Waggoner Kidnapping Case." August 23, 1860.

*Cincinnati (OH) Enquirer.* "$50 Reward." May 15, 1841.

————. "A Fugitive-Slave Case." October 29, 1859.

————. "The Fugitive Slave Case." January 31, 1856.

————. "Remanding of a Fugitive Slave." April 4, 1861.

*Cincinnati (OH) Gazette.* "Three Slaves Taken by Habeas Corpus." August 27, 1853.

*Cleveland (OH) Daily Leader.* "Another Exploit of U.S. Deputy Marshal Manson Among the Negroes." October 16, 1860.

———. "Pious Kidnapper Jennings Claims Him!" July 4, 1860.

———. "The Sandusky Kidnapping Case." October 17, 1860.

*Cleveland (OH) Morning Leader.* "The Kidnapping Case—Conductor Sherman." October 18, 1860.

Cochran, William Cox. "Oberlin-Wellington Rescue Case." *The Western Reserve and the Fugitive Slave Law*, Transactions: The Western Reserve Historical Society, No. 101, January 1920.

Cox, Fred E., John Randolph and John Harris. "The Jugbands of Louisville." *Storyville No. 155*, September 1, 1993.

Crenshaw, Gwendolyn J. *Bury Me in a Free Land.* Indianapolis: Indiana Historical Bureau, 1993.

Crigler, Alberta Hale. "Justice for Former Slaves 162 Years Later." *Daily Press* (Victorville, CA), April 10, 2012.

Day, Michelle A., and Joseph Wickens. "The Arrest and Trial of Lucy Bagby." *Cleveland Historical.* Accessed June 10, 2020. https://clevelandhistorical.org/items/show/517.

*Delaware (OH) Gazette.* "More Kidnapping." November 18, 1859.

*The Delaware Register or Farmers', Manufacturers' and Mechanics Advocate.* August 15, 1829.

*Democrat and Herald* (Wilmington, OH). "Abduction Case." November 20, 1840.

*Detroit (MI) Free Press.* "The Late Fugitive Slave Case at Zanesville, Ohio." May 13, 1859.

"Driskell v. Parish." *Western Law Journal* 5, no. 5 (1848).

*Eaton (OH) Democrat.* "Another Fugitive Slave Case." June 18, 1857.

*Evansville (IN) Daily Journal.* "The Fugitive Slave Case." June 4, 1857.

*Evening Post* (New York). "Abolition in Cincinnati." July 2, 1841.

*Fremont (OH) Weekly Journal.* "Another Slave Case." May 6, 1859.

———. "Kidnapping at Columbus." November 4, 1859.

*Gallipolis (OH) Journal.* "Fugitive Slave Case." August 25, 1853.

*Green-Mountain Freeman* (Montpelier, VT). "Samuel Watson." February 28, 1845.

Hale, James L. "The Famous Negro Polley Family of Lawrence County, Part 1." *Herald-Dispatch* (Huntington, WV), October 8, 2014.

The Heritage Guide to the Constitution. "Fugitive Slave Clause." Accessed October 10, 2019. https://www.heritage.org/constitution/#!/articles/4/essays/124/fugitive-slave-clause.

*Highland (OH) Weekly News.* "Supposed Kidnapping Case." July 5, 1860.

*Hillsdale (MI) Standard.* "Look-out Slaveholders." November 30, 1852.

History. "Salmon P. Chase." Accessed October 8, 2019. https://www.history.com/topics/us-government/salmon-p-chase.

*Holmes County (OH) Farmer.* "The Iberia Outrage." December 27, 1860.

*Holmes County (OH) Republican.* "The Fugitive Slave Case." May 12, 1859.

———. "Kidnapping at Columbus." November 10, 1859.

———. "Remarks of Rev. George Gordon to the U.S. Court." December 19, 1861.

House Divided Project. "Dickinson and Slavery." Accessed May 21, 2021. https://housedivided.dickinson.edu/sites/slavery/people/richard-mcallister/.

*Huron (OH) Reflector.* "Kidnapping! Dating Outrage!" April 7, 1846.

Hylton, J. Gordon. "Before There Were 'Red' and 'Blue' States." *Marquette University Law School Faculty Blog,* December 20, 2012. Accessed May 7, 2021. https://law.marquette.edu/facultyblog/2012/12/before-there-were-red-and-blue-states-there-were-free-states-and-slave-states/comment-page-1/.

*Ironton (OH) Register.* "Gov. Dennison's Message Relating to the Polly Negro Family." February 2, 1860.

Jefferson Quotes & Family Letters. "Extract from Thomas Jefferson to Joel Yancey." Accessed June 18, 2020. http://tjrs.monticello.org/letter/2117.

Kahn, Andrew, and Jamelle Bouie. "The Atlantic Slave Trade in Tow Minutes." Slate. Accessed July 6, 2018. http://www.slate.com/articles/life/the_history_of_american_slavery/2015/06/animated_interactive_of_the_history_of_the_atlantic_slave_trade.html.

*The Liberator* (Boston, MA). "Another Fugitive Slave Case." April 29, 1859.

———. "The Case of Charles Waggoner." September 28, 1860.

———. "Escape of an Alleged Fugitive." October 28, 1853.

———. "The Human Sacrifice!" March 8, 1861.

———. "A Mob in Cincinnati." July 16, 1841.

———. "Slave Case." June 22, 1838.

Lincoln, Abraham. "The Emancipation Proclamation." National Archives. Accessed June 10, 2020. https://www.archives.gov/exhibits/featured-documents/emancipation-proclamation/transcript.html.

*Louisville (KY) Daily Courier.* "Fugitive Slave Case in Cincinnati." October 20, 1853.

———. "Important Slave Case Decision." January 16, 1851.

"The Massachusetts Body of Liberties." Accessed July 7, 2018. https://history.hanover.edu/texts/masslib.html.

McNutt, Randy. "New Richmond Marker Recalls Slavery Opposition." *Cincinnati Enquirer*, February 8, 2003.

Meigs, Return Jonathan, Jr. "Judges Supreme Court State of Ohio." *Medico-Legal Journal* 18, supplement (1900).

"Miller v. McQuerry." Accessed July 4, 2020. https://law.resource.org/pub/us/case/reporter/F.Cas/0017.f.cas/0017.f.cas.0335.pdf.

*The National Era* (Washingon, D.C.). "Rev. Henry Dennison's Slave Girl." April 5, 1855.

*New York Herald*. "Arrest and Examination of Eight Fugitive Slaves in Cincinnati." June 19, 1854.

*New York Tribune*. "The Fugitive Slave Case in Zanesville." May 10, 1859.

———. "A Kidnapping Case." March 7, 1851.

*Niles National Register* (St. Louis, MO). "No Slavery in Ohio." May 29, 1841.

———. "Western Law." June 5, 1841.

"The Northwest Ordinance (1787)." Accessed July 20, 2019. https://usa.usembassy.de/etexts/democrac/5.htm.

Ohio County Public Library. "Biography: Sara Lucy Bagby." https://www.ohiocountylibrary.org/wheeling-history/biography-sara-lucy-bagby/4287. Accessed July 11, 2020.

Ohio Historical Society. "Case of Polly Negroes Memorandum." Peyton Polly Collection, 1856–1859. Accessed June 12, 2020. http://dbs.ohiohistory.org/africanam/html/mss/vfm3627.html.

———. "Ralph Seete to Governor Salmon P. Chase, July 25, 1856." Peyton Polly Collection, 1856–1859. Accessed June 12, 2020. http://dbs.ohiohistory.org/africanam/html/mss/vfm3627.html.

Pocock, Emil. "Slavery and Freedom in the Early Republic." *Ohio Valley History* 6, no. 1 (Spring 2006).

*Pomeroy (OH) Weekly Telegraph*. "Is This a Civilized County?" June 12, 1860.

*Portage (OH) Sentinel*. "The Other Side." April 15, 1846.

*Prairie News* (Okolona, MS). "The Fugitive Slave Law." July 14, 1859.

*Randolph Journal* (Winchester, IN). "Attempt to Capture Bracken County Slaves." October 4, 1860.

———. "Trial of Wm. M. Connelly." May 13, 1858.

"The Real Justice Taney." *Wilson Quarterly*, Fall 2010. Accessed June 29, 2018. https://www.wilsonquarterly.com/quarterly/fall-2010-what-if-china-fails/the-real-justice-taney/.

*The Republic* (Washington, D.C.). "The Underground Railroad." November 22, 1852.

*Richmond (VA) Dispatch*. "Fugitive Slave Case." October 24, 1853.

"Salmon Portland Chase." *Ohio Law Reporter* 3, no. 34 (December 1905).

*Sandusky (OH) Clarion.* "Boys Claimed as Fugitive Slaves." March 8, 1845.

Siebert, Wilbur. "Major E.D. Caws and Mr. Ealy Account of a Fugitive-Slave Catcher." Wilbur H. Siebert Underground Railroad Collection. Accessed July 19, 2020. https://www.ohiomemory.org/digital/collection/siebert/id/7857/rec/7.

Sloane, Rush R. "The Underground Railroad of the Firelands." *The Firelands Pioneer*, July 1888.

Smith, William Henry. "The First Fugitive Slave Case of Record in Ohio." In *Annual Report of the American Historical Association, The Year 1893.* Washington, D.C.: Government Printing Office, 1894.

Stafford, Tom. "Clark County Sheriff Was Felled by Federal Marshals." *Springfield (OH) News-Sun*, June 2, 2013.

*Summit County (OH) Beacon.* "Return of Mr. Welton." February 6, 1862.

The Supreme Court of Ohio and the Ohio Judicial System. "John McLean." Accessed June 24, 2020. https://www.supremecourt.ohio.gov/SCO/formerjustices/bios/mclean.asp.

Taylor, Nikki. "Reconsidering the 'Forced' Exodus of 1829." *Journal of African American History* 87 (Summer 2002).

*Weekly Marysville (OH) Tribune.* "Honor to Whom Honor Is Due." June 28, 1854.

Wright, Florence Bedford. "A Station on the Underground Railroad." *Ohio Archaeological and Historical Society Publications* 14 (1906).

*Zanesville (OH) Courier.* "Fugitive Slave Case." February 17, 1851.

———. "The Ohio Legislature Advised." January 5, 1861.

# INDEX

# V

# ABOUT THE AUTHORS

A graduate of Miami and Ohio State Universities, David Meyers has written a number of local histories, as well as several novels and works for the stage. He was recently inducted into the Ohio Senior Citizens Hall of Fame for his contributions to local history.

Elise Meyers Walker is a graduate of Hofstra University and Ohio University. She has collaborated with her father on a dozen local histories, including *Ohio's Black Hand Syndicate*, *Lynching and Mob Violence in Ohio* and *A Murder in Amish Ohio*. They are both available for interviews, book signings and presentations.

The authors' website is www.explodingstove.com or follow them on Facebook, Twitter, Instagram, YouTube and RedBubble at @explodingstove.

*Visit us at*
www.historypress.com
.................................................................